ANARCHIST STUDIES

Volume 17 Number 1

99a Wallis Road, London E9 5LN
www.lwbooks.co.uk
info@lwbooks.co.uk
tel 020 8533 2506

ISSN 0976 3393

For information on submitting contributions to Anarchist Studies please visit our website at www.lwbooks.co.uk/anarchiststudies

Subscriptions
2009 subscriptions are (for two issues):
Personal £20
Institutional £52

Typeset by E-Type, Liverpool
Cover illustration: lc-mihrak, 'World Riot', 2009, digital graphic © lc-mihrak.

Anarchist Studies is indexed in Alternative Press Index, British Humanities Index, CIRA, Left Index, International Bibliography of the Social Sciences, Sociological Abstracts and *Sonances*

Printed in Great Britain by the MPG Books Group, Bodmin and King's Lynn

Contents

'World Riot' is by the Turkish anarchist collective 'iç-mihrak'. Ic-mihrak ('internal focus') is a term Turkish nationalists use to define domestic groups engaged in so-called treason, with or without foreign support. Ic-mihrak have adopted it as an ironic transgression of any established cultural/political nomos, be it legal, political, traditional, popular, humanistic, secular or religious.

Iç-mihrak is an Istanbul cultural intervention collective founded in 2007. It operates as a non-hierarchical, anti-authoritarian consensus-based 'semiotic-terrorism' group, utilising street stickers, web blogs, and any other means of disturbing the peace. Contorting, distorting and inverting official, popular and traditional cultural epistemes, iç-mihrak presents texts and images that interrupt statist logic autonomously, without the mediation of the art world.

Members of iç-mihrak define themselves as anarchist activists making use of visual arts as a method of struggle to reclaim and defend cultural territory against exploitation by the state and its official and unofficial apparatus. Iç-mihrak does not politicise art, it invokes art as one of many forms of resistance.

Iç-mihrak strives for a high-quality aesthetic unencumbered by negation and resentment. Knowing that mockery is what rulers fear the most, the collective laughs hysterically at the cultural codes sustaining state power.

The ape-like cops in 'World Riot' advance against a slogan 'You can kill the Protestor/You can't kill the Protest'. 'World Riot' is dedicated to all dead activists in the name of Alexis Grigoropoulos.

Anarchist Studies 17.1 © 2009 ISSN 0976 3393
www.lwbooks.co.uk/journals/anarchiststudies/

Editorial

Ruth Kinna

This year is the two-hundredth anniversary of Proudhon's birth and, though he remains a controversial figure, it seems fitting to mark the occasion. Proudhon is often remembered for his anti-Semitism and his anti-feminism, charges which are difficult to deny. Critics have also traditionally accused him of individualism and idealism – usually without explaining why these traits should be treated negatively. Stirner accused him of confusion, though his objection that the concept of theft required prior validation of a concept of property perhaps overlooked the distinction between dominion and use that lay at the heart of Proudhon's critique. Another well-aired criticism is that Proudhon chose a poor epithet to describe his thought: why call yourself an anarchist when anarchy is understood to mean chaos, disorder and social malaise? Can't the confusions of anarchism with the chaos of anarchy be laid at Proudhon's door?

One response to this objection is that Proudhon's selection of the A-word to describe his politics did not confuse ideas about anarchism – and nor could it have done, since the ideas themselves had not been articulated. Moreover, when it came to exposition, Proudhon wrote with confidence that the contradictions that dogged mainstream thinking about centrally-managed polities were plain to see – or could be laid bare – and that the alternatives, the lines of which he carefully delineated, were clearly better. His position was assertive rather than defensive. Of course, this tradition is still well-represented in modern writing. Nevertheless, it's surprising how many would-be defenders of anarchism reinforce the very images they seek to contest, by taking the ideas of the opposition as a starting-point for discussion.

The articles in this issue cover considerable ground: from contemporary politics to the working of finance capital, the intersection of anarchism and art and the history of anarchist utopianism. The opening pieces are short reflections –

opinion pieces, expressing a range of views and from different standpoints – on recent events in Gaza and Greece. In the three substantive essays, Guido Preparata provides a comprehensive guide to the global economic system and the US Treasury's place within it – a prelude to a companion piece that will appear in Issue 18.1. Peter Wilkin's discussion of Tory anarchism examines an anarchistic satirical tradition in British thought and uses the analysis to reflect on British identity and the role of the empire in its construction. Ginger Frost's essay looks at the idea of free love and the attempt of early twentieth-century anarchists to live the principle in a hostile world. Gustave Courbet's decision to paint out Proudhon's wife and replace her with a basket suggests that Proudhon would not have been impressed with such radical behaviours – but that's just one recommendation.

Sharp-eyed readers will have noticed the new format and cover design for AS – thanks are due to all at Lawrence and Wishart for working on the new look.

Happy Birthday Proudhon!

Anarchist Studies 17.1 © 2009 ISSN 0976 3393
www.lwbooks.co.uk/journals/anarchiststudies/

Facts on the ground

Uri Gordon

The watchword on the streets was: 'The landlord's gone crazy'. The goal of the operation: 'To fuck their mothers' mother'. Calls to erase Gaza rode lightly off people's lips. Hamas are armed and dangerous. Destroy their buildings, their personnel. Anyone around them is as good as dead.

Since the end of the 2006 Lebanon War, the expectation of a future 'big operation in Gaza' that would restore the muddied honour of the Israeli army has been periodically floated in the media, and normalised in Israelis' consciousness. On the day after the US elections, Israel was the first to break the elapsed ceasefire with Hamas, which in response renewed its own rocket attacks. In truth, Israel had never kept its side of the Egyptian-brokered bargain over the ceasefire, in failing to end the harsh economic blockade.

A Russian joke: 'They told me, 'Relax, it could be worse'. So I relaxed, and indeed it got worse.'

As Qassam attacks by Hamas or some other Gazan militia inevitably continue throughout the aerial bombardment, the army moves to Stage Two. A column cuts through the middle of the Gaza Strip. Advance positions are taken. Yet the opponent fails to come out fighting. And so the living city is rent asunder, in a war-game with no strategic objective, only to spend ammunition looking for the enemy with zero casualties. As they tunnel their way through living-room walls into Gaza City, Israeli conscripts throw explosives ahead to protect themselves from possible ambushes and mines. Hamas store weapons in mosques and apartment buildings and carry out dozens of punishment beatings on alleged collaborators. Most of the dead are civilians, maybe a third are children. Thousands of homes are destroyed. Ambulances and hospitals are fired upon.

Meanwhile, on the other side of the 10 metre-high walls that surround Gaza,

Israeli war-resisters meet a brick wall everywhere they turn. Jewish Israelis have a knee-jerk nationalist loyalty when they perceive Israel is being attacked.

The response is essentially: What do these bleeding-heart peaceniks expect us to do when we are attacked? They didn't protest Hamas's rockets which have been pounding Israel for the past eight years whilst the children in Sderot wet their beds in fear (Sderot is the Israeli town next to Gaza which has suffered most from Hamas rocket attacks). What do these Europeans know? They just hate Israel and Israelis and don't think our lives are worth anything. All the hatred in demonstrations against Israel across Europe, with calls to kill the Jews, just shows me that, if we don't protect ourselves no one else will come to Israel's defence.

The fears of annihilation, fed by well-fanned collective trauma, are close to the surface and easily manipulated by politicians and pundits. Dehumanisation of the enemy helps explain the simple indifference to the shameless attacks on Palestinians in Gaza by all three major candidates in the recent elections.

In the name of the Jews, the Israeli state drives Palestinians from their lands, imprisons them and punishes them with blundering brutality. The Revisionist policy dreamed up by early fascist Zionists of 'Facts on the Ground' is a total success – Israel's perceived choice today is between Apartheid and ethnic cleansing. The Israeli elections have seen the meteoric rise of Avigdor Leiberman, whose party, Israel Beitenu, promises to strip Palestinian citizens of Israel and Leftists of their citizenship if they fail tests of loyalty to the state. This isn't swear-word fascism – this is the real thing. Still on the table is Kadima's 'realignment' plan to withdraw Israeli settlers from the 'Palestinian' side of the segregation barrier. This is a de-facto annexation of six per-cent of West Bank territory, which, crucially, would leave it in two landlocked islands, an internal enemy non-state which can now be disciplined on the same terms as Gaza.

The last six decades have seen the (at least) fifth ethnic cleansing event to take place on this soil. But so far it has been ethnic cleansing with somewhere to run. In Gaza it was verging on something different. The Gaza war was an intentional threat to commit ethnic cleansing with nowhere to run. The Israeli state was threatening to commit genocide and everybody knew it.

As if anyone still needed proof that an unspeakable blasphemy is being acted out without restraint in the Middle East. A twisted logic allows the Holocaust to become not a warning-post against brutal authority, but the relevant upper limit for the defensible actions of the state that alleges to act on behalf of its victims. And even if you convinced Israelis to see through all that, they would still have no framework for taking action.

No, that's not true. There are some things we can do – go to demonstrations (but you have to have some courage, as you get heckled and eggs and water thrown at you. When anarchists did a vigil in Tel Aviv, even firemen stopped to turn a hose on them). Or take symbolic direct action (twenty-one arrested and held on 'secret intelligence' that their lawyer was not allowed to see). Take blankets to the Red Crescent (the convoy of ten truckloads of emergency supplies sent by Israeli citizens to Gaza was turned back. The radio falsely reported that the aid was let through). Even this most humane action elicits angry cries of one-sidedness – and what about the kids in Sderot?

Sadly, Israelis show little interest in noting that not all the kids in Sderot are willing to be their excuse. There is a project in Sderot called Kol Akher ('Another Voice'). For the past year, the members have been in telephone contact with residents of Gaza, trying to make a personal connection between them and the residents of Sderot. Even during the war, the contact was not broken. They believe that, if the residents of Gaza and Sderot can put a human face to the enemy, it will be more difficult for the leaders in the region to choose the path of violence.

These are the only victories, really. Not pro-Israel or pro-Palestine but pro-a just and lasting peace based on the principles of co-operation and friendship between the peoples that live in these lands. We have to defy our corrupt leaders and the narratives that they want us to believe, and show another way is possible and that the hatred and endless violence cannot continue ... We just wish there were more of us.

Anarchist Studies 17.1 © 2009 ISSN 0976 3393
www.lwbooks.co.uk/journals/anarchiststudies/

The aftermaths of the war on Gaza

Osama Abu-Irshaid

After twenty-two days of unprecedented attacks on Gaza, Israel announced a unilateral cease-fire. Over 1300 Palestinians were killed and more than 5300 injured. Approximately a third of those killed and injured were women and children. According to Palestinian sources in Gaza the majority of victims of the Israel aggression were unarmed civilians.

Israel announced a series of objectives at the beginning of the war. It stated that it wanted to prevent primitive Palestinian rockets from reaching its southern towns. It also sought to weaken Hamas rule in Gaza and bring down its government. The hope was that the Gaza Strip would revert back to Palestinian Authority control led by President Mamoud Abbas (Abu Mazen). There was talk of freeing the captured Israeli soldier Gilad Schalit whom Hamas had captured and has been holding for over two and a half years. In exchange for Israeli demands for his release Hamas has demanded the release of hundreds of Palestinian prisoners.

After three weeks of sustained aggression Israel was unable to achieve any of its goals. Rockets continued to fall on Israeli towns in the south. The last rockets launched were contemporaneous with the writing of this article. In addition, Hamas has emerged once more the de facto and sole authority in Gaza. Finally, Hamas still holds Schalit.

Though Israel announced a unilateral cease-fire and has withdrawn its forces from the Strip, it has been compelled to continue talks in Cairo to find ways of reaching a mutual calm again with Hamas. The last cease-fire lasted six months, between June and December of 2008. This time, Israel sought to forbid Hamas from claiming a political victory – as it did once before – that the cease-fire had been reached by mutual agreement. However, once again it is clear that calm cannot be achieved without Hamas. Therefore, Hamas today has declared victory in enduring the onslaught of a vastly superior Israeli military machine. Apart from securing open terrain, Israeli forces did not venture to overtake the highly populated areas where Hamas fighters and the other Palestinian resistance were lying in wait.

On 27 January 2009 an Israeli patrol was attacked within Gaza's borders by the Palestinian resistance. An Israeli soldier was killed and three were injured by the detonation of an explosive. In retaliation, Israel bombed cites inside the Strip, killing a police officer and injuring eighteen civilians, among them eleven school children. In a further response, Palestinian rockets were launched anew into southern Israel. Israel now threatens to escalate its attacks. In other words, at the time of writing we are on the verge of a new cycle of violence. The prospect reinforces the claim that there can be no solution to the situation in Gaza without the involvement of Hamas.

The movement has been emboldened by the indispensable role it has played. It feels it had achieved a victory in not having been defeated. These claims are justified to the extent Hamas that continues to function and act as a spoiler. Despite the heavy price exacted on Hamas and the population in the military campaign, the brutality of the pictures emanating from Gaza have garnered world sympathy for the Palestinians and inflamed anger against Israel. Israel lost the public relations campaign. It did not succeed in portraying the campaign as a war on terror since it was clear that the vast majority of victims have been unarmed civilians, especially women and children.

Hamas has benefited from the brutality of Israeli violence against Palestinian civilians. The movement no longer needs to substantiate the claim that Israel engages in 'state terrorism' against unarmed civilians living under its occupation. Palestinians, among them Hamas, have always argued that the Israeli state is based on terrorism and ethnic cleansing. The refugee issue has been one aspect of the policy of massacres committed against the Palestinians by Zionist gangs, predating the establishment of Israel and continuing in the present day. In the past, technology was not sufficiently advanced to record the process step by step, but the Gaza massacre has vindicated Palestinian claims about the nature of Israel.

Hamas also benefited ideologically as an organisation in the minds of Palestinians, Arabs and Muslims. Hamas' steadfastness in facing for three weeks what is considered one of the most powerful armies in the world is a source of enormous respect. Hezbollah's reputation was similarly enhanced when it stood up to Israel in

South Lebanon in the sum
position was more precari
Hamas was fighting w
difficulty. They did not h
air and sea. Their fighters
Nor did they have access
revolutionary guard. In 2
as it received support fro
the war. Hamas and the c
which does not exceed 3
under a punishing siege a
a half years Gaza has bee
gling. In fact everything
blockaded, undermining
geographical allies like S
with necessities throughout the war of 2006. As for Egypt, if anything, it was hostile to Hamas. It feared having on its borders what it considers to be an ideological affiliate of Egypt's strongest opposition party, the Muslim Brotherhood. Against these odds, the Palestinian, Arab and Muslim masses viewed Hamas as the symbolic 'Palestinian David' standing up to Israel the 'Jewish Goliath'.

On the ideological level, the sheer destruction and brutality inflicted on Gaza and its population of 1.5 million residents has strengthened those in Hamas who argue that coexistence with Israel is impossible. In the period before the mid-1990s the official rhetoric of Hamas changed from the language of a religiously-based conflict with the Jews (reflected in the Hamas Charter published in 1988) to a politically-inspired discourse of national liberation, which identified Israel as an enemy not because of its Jewish character but because it is an occupying power. Now, although it is not new to hear voices in both the Jewish and Muslim communities arguing that this is essentially a religious conflict that cannot be resolved, unfortunately the rhetoric of religious difference has increased on the Palestinian, Arab and Muslim side. The crimes that were committed in Gaza have caused many Arabs and Muslims to revert to institutionalised religious language based on their understanding of Qur'anic, prophetic and historical texts about the eternal struggle between Islam and Judaism, Muslims

logy about a war ending the world, and

me.

t to weaken Hamas. The policy has been coun-

Israeli war against the movement – attempting to

n, blockade it, assassinate its leaders, and destroy its

ement has grown in stature. With this war Arab officialdom

o camps. One camp, led by Egypt and Saudi Arabia, sought to

r the war and attempted to isolate it and weaken it. The other

Syria and Qatar, sought to bolster and support Hamas' position, if

tically – and this minimal support went a long way to strengthen Hamas'

e. Now Hamas not only has popular legitimacy, it also has new official Arab

gitimacy, at least amongst a segment of Arab opinion. The Arab summit held in Doha, Qatar on 16 January 2009 was boycotted by a number of Arab states and the PLO, but it was attended by several others and Hamas' Bureau Chief sat at the same table as Arab leaders, alongside other leaders of the Palestinian resistance.

Even the official Arab opposition to Hamas, specifically Egypt, has been obliged to recognise the centrality of Hamas and its role in any future ceasefire talks with Israel. This is the conclusion that some European powers have reached, and secret channels of communication have been opened with the movement. It appears that the new American Democratic administration headed by President Barack Obama is coming to this view. Former President Jimmy Carter, who is close to Obama, has pushed for talks with Hamas. The appointment of George Mitchell as Special Envoy to the Middle East, known for his pragmatism and balanced approach, is quite possibly a reflection of this new American advance and it may bear fruit. It is interesting to note that the Mitchell appointment was opposed by strong voices within the US-Israeli lobby, precisely because he holds views about the necessity of incorporating Hamas; views that America must respect if their role as honest broker in the Middle East conflict is to be sustained.

Everybody talks about the need for a 'secure Israel' as a premise for peace in the region. And some talk about the necessity of establishing a contiguous Palestinian state conducive to normal life and natural development as a precondition. But in all this, there is no getting away from the fact that the real tension in the region is due to the Israeli occupation. Israel is occupying Palestine. Hamas and the other resistance groups are nothing more than a reaction to this illegal occupation.

Without a viable Palestinian state and Palestinian self-determination there will be no peace in the region. Hamas is a manifestation of Israeli oppression. The latest legislative elections indicate and clarify that Palestinians yearn for the day of liberation that Hamas is promising. In the meantime, Israel, through its occupation and criminal violations of international law and its blockade of Gaza and its people, increases hatred against it in the region and the world at large.

Israel did not win the campaign, and Hamas did not lose it. The future is bleak for Israel if it continues to occupy Palestine and insist on denying Palestinians their aspirations for freedom, liberation and the opportunity to express a legitimate national will. Unfortunately, until Israel recognises this, there will be no real peace even if the adversaries manage to conclude another truce of one, two or even ten years.

Anarchist Studies 17.1 © 2009 ISSN 0976 3393
www.lwbooks.co.uk/journals/anarchiststudies/

'We wish you a merry crisis and a happy new fear'

A postscript from the December riots in Athens

Christos Iliopoulos

On 6 December a policeman shot and killed a 15-year-old boy in Exarchia, a region of Athens well known for its grass-roots libertarianism. Within a few hours the whole city was being burnt down by hordes of furious protesters whose targets were of anti-capitalist, anti-state and anti-commercial significance: banks, car trade companies, big stores, ministries, police stations, even the huge Christmas tree in Syntagma square. The riots continued for almost three days, with the conflict between the protesters and the forces of repression taking place on the streets among burning buildings and barricades.

Many tried to find a parallel between these riots and recent events in the French suburbs or even with the events of May '68. Although the causes and reasons for such outbreaks seem quite similar, the case of Athens must be seen separately for it differs in one basic point: those who participated in the assaults in Athens were not only university students, labourers or immigrants. They were from all of the above groups and even more: school pupils, middle-aged bourgeois, people with or without a political background and consciousness – all fed up with high rates of unemployment, poverty, state murders, repression and violence; with consumer standards of living and urban isolation. Moreover, the persistence of many academics – veterans of the '68 conflicts – to negatively compare these days to their own, showing an elitist stance towards the protesters, caused an angry reaction, expressed in seemingly apolitical slogans like 'Fuck May '68 – Fight Now!' or 'You demolished our lives, we'll demolish everything!'

What conclusions can be drawn from the riots and what is the significance of this mobilisation for the Greek radical movement?

First, there is a question of definition. Revolution or Revolt? As Max Stirner put it, revolution is an iconoclastic process driven by a desire to substitute the old 'idols' with new ones. In contrast, through revolt the ego is trying to retrieve all the things stolen from it. From that point of view those burning days of December were not a revolution but a pure revolt. This conclusion takes us to a dual critical point – that is, the internal and external significance of these days for the radicals in Greece.

The internal component has to do with the movement itself. It's been a long time since anarchist, anti-authoritarian and autonomous activists were praised by 'mainstream' civilians and a significant percentage of the public opinion. It seems that the most hard-core and radical parts of Greek political life have renewed their bonds with society despite the constant, negative state propaganda. In addition, all the squats, the marches, the assemblies and the general alternative action which took place in the name of this revolt generated new expectations and responsibilities. It's high time that radical factions dealt with the anti-capitalist and anti-state struggles in even more consistent and organised ways – beyond violent means.

The external component concerns the emancipation of the protest movement from the custody of the parliamentary left. Orthodox communists as well as Euro-communists and the rest of the alternative but parliamentary left were totally incapable of taking control of this sweeping action. Their Marxist, 'scientific' tools of historical analysis could neither predict nor explain the revolutionary orgasm that hit Athens (and many other Greek cities). As a result, the Greek Communist Party started talking about provocateurs who sabotage the goals of the working class whilst the Radical Left League was making ambiguous statements in order to gain as many votes as possible for the oncoming elections.

Athens' recent revolt has a lot to teach every European – and not only European – radical social movement about direct action, without avant-gardes and representatives, which will constitute the first step against capitalism and the state, without regard to their abolition. After all, as Errico Malatesta put it: 'We will not reach anarchy neither today nor tomorrow nor in ten centuries. We walk towards anarchy today, tomorrow, always ...'

Anarchist Studies 17.1 © 2009 ISSN 0976 3393
www.lwbooks.co.uk/journals/anarchiststudies/

Of money, heresy, and surrender

Part I: The ways of our system, an outline, from Bretton Woods to the financial slump of 2008

Guido Giacomo Preparata

Associate Professor of Political Economy
University of Washington (2000-2008)

ggprep@yahoo.com

ABSTRACT

This is the first of a two-part study of a fundamental but neglected truth concerning the nature of money. Pushing alone against the doctrinaire cross-currents of the monetary maelstrom, anarchist reformers have since the 1920s discussed the introduction of *time-dated money*. The institutional and theoretical issues underpinning this revolutionary innovation, as well as the questions of its workability in the contemporary framework, will be presented in *Anarchist Studies* 18.1 (2010). The present article prefaces this extraordinarily important chapter of reformist thought by providing a summary historical account of the monetary system in which we live. This is done with a view to casting in relief the intimately dysfunctional and inequitable constitution of the latter and to contemplate how a blueprint for communal reform based on the principle of perishable money may correct such wrongs.

Key words *Money, policy, empire, United States, business cycle, finance, economic history*

INTRODUCTION

It has been the exclusive merit of the German communal/anarchist thinkers of the 1920s, namely Silvio Gesell (1864-1930) and Rudolf Steiner (1861-1925) to have conceived and articulated the genial idea of overcoming the chief obstacles strewn along the distributive chain of the economy by means of a *time-sensitive money certificate*. The logic supporting the concept is, in fact, straightforward: Gesell and Steiner reasoned that if it is agreed that 1) money is indeed a symbolic medium –perfected with the sole aim of expediting exchange, and that 2) such an exchange is between goods (and services), which perforce are (or rely on means and resources that are) *perishable*, then it must logically follow that the key to a wholesome arrangement of productive factors and remunerative flows should itself be boosted by a form of money bearing an expiration date. In other words, simple economics demands that money die.

The political consequences that would arise from the implementation of such an intuition are momentous: it is clear that a reform of this sort would definitely encroach upon the privileges of the banking industry, which is the most guarded and powerful oligopoly of all. Incidentally, the legitimacy of this cartel on the one hand, and American hegemony on the other, are two of the chief tenets of orthodox western ideology: all western practitioners of the social sciences that wish to advance in the incumbent power structure know that these are never to be questioned overtly – i.e. pricked in their neuralgic nodes. Among other aspects of the question, this essay will show how these two articles of modern political faith (money and US primacy) are intimately tied, so much that, as evidenced by the recent crisis, it is nearly impossible to discuss national monetary/economic issues – European or otherwise – without making constant referrals to the role of the United States.

How then would the privileged position of banking be threatened by time-dated certificates or virtual renditions thereof? The bulk of what we call money is put into existence, not by central banks – which act as issuing appendices of this complex amalgam of private and public affairs – but by the private banking network itself through a systematic process of 'mortgaging' (or wealth, income, etc). In other terms, commercial banks derive their power from the license, which states grant them, to manufacture money by way of loans, a process which is itself enabled by the management of virtual ciphers (money) that never die. By grace of this monetary *hoard*, which by definition may be withheld whenever investment prospects are not deemed promising, and by grace of their control over a vast network of payments, credit institutes have from time immemorial exacted from the body economic copious rents (interest charges), which make them the force they are. 'Hoard' is the key word in this case. If perishable money, which carries the anti-hoarding device in the expiration date, were injected into the productive fabric of society, it would outflank the banking network by spurring a circuit of its own – one where banks would on the one hand inevitably, and justly, surrender a sizeable measure of decisional clout to the productive sector, and on the other, no longer base their investment policies on mere interest-driven exigencies. Clearly, a growing share of business conducted outside the conventional perimeter of banking represents for the latter lost interest as well as diminished influence.

That this isn't a quixotic theme with merely utopian aspirations is attested by the non-peripheral and serious discussion of Gesell's reformist agenda that took place in mainstream academia during the Depression (the most famous interventions thereon being those by J. M. Keynes and Irving Fisher, which will be briefly discussed in Part II). More recently (2006), evidence of perishable money's power of suggestion is afforded by the uneasy reaction on the part of Germany's central bank to a flurry of regional movements intent on availing themselves of time-sensitive media of payment. As will be recounted in Part II, initiatives to realise regional associations of exchange and development by means of time-dated money have been afoot for several years all over the world. These have remained to this day largely circumscribed for a variety of reasons, but the fact that they do exist, that they have made such a notable comeback along with a resurgent interest in the figures of Gesell and the economics of Steiner, is sufficient proof that there is something of abiding value and wisdom in the underlying idea.

Before discussing the challenges associated with the promotion of a tool and a conception as unconventional as time-sensitive money (which is the main subject of Part II), it is appropriate to offer – as this first instalment is designed to do – a chronological sketch of the monetary environment that we inhabit: the system whose institutions we wish to modify. As shall be argued, the picture that offers itself in the west is one characterised by the imbalances engendered by conventional banking at the domestic (national) level – difficulties roughly identical for the economies of all countries which, in the post-second world war era, have become inextricably enmeshed in the tangle of America's imperial goals. The latter aspect is the specific focus of this essay.

Presently, we have reached a situation of substantial complexity. In its essential traits, however, it amounts roughly to a modernised replica of the late Roman imperial arrangement. What we are lately dealing with is a set-up whereby the imperial centre, having dismantled its manufactures over the course of the past generation, has eventually found itself functioning as the world's virtual marketplace. It stands willingly as the 'number one' globalised market venue of the world, propped by an array of service industries (e.g. commerce and transportation), led in turn by the executive strategies of the financial sector: at the basic operational level, think of the American economy as an expanded, world-wide E-bay store with its associated financial arm, Paypal, deputised to dispatch the money flows accompanying trillion dollars' worth of transactions (financial and otherwise). The economies of the world are 'moored' as it were to the US market by means of the latter's openness to their exports (China's above all). The underlying design is subtle: in order to bind the vassal economies of the world to their global emporium, the economic capital of the empire, New York, moves to attract the savings of the world, which are subsequently disposed of to cover the budget and trade deficits. In other words, foreigners are invited to invest in the USA, which employs such capital flows to cover the cost, inter alia, of military expenditures and the (imported) commodities it no longer needs to produce; determined to impede a rapid appreciation of their currencies, the foreign vassals find themselves forced to 'reinvest' the dollar proceeds obtained from their export sales to the United States in American securities. Thus, banking on its dollar, which the world hoards as the chief 'reserve currency,' the United States has managed to harness to its financial engine the productive apparatuses of the world, which have been locked into the imperial system via the lure of appealing yields on Wall Street and the concomitant 'concession' to offer a wide range of goods for sale on the American marketplace. The locomotive of this massively unwholesome construction is Wall Street itself, upon whose creative finance the imperial elite of Washington DC relies in order to set the world caravan in motion. In such a setting – the so-called neo-liberal order (post 1979) – the inflation of speculative bubbles is a functional necessity. Thus far the system has experienced three such five-to-six year speculative cycles: the Volcker/Reagan stock market jolt of the 1980s (1982-87), Greenspan's historical dot.com boom (1994-2000), and Bush Junior's subprime mortgage-fest (2002-2007), at whose trough we now find ourselves.

FROM THE TRADITIONAL BOOM/BUST TANDEM OF BIG BUSINESS TO THE 'SERIAL BUBBLE DEPENDENCY' OF THE 'NEW ECONOMY'

> Bubbles, excess and calamity are part of the package of Western finance. And still it is worth it.
>
> *The Economist*[1]

1. Business enterprise in a nutshell …

How does the capitalist machine function under the regime of imperishable money? The answer is: by spurts, by alternate bouts of panic and elation. The banks' interest rate always bides its time: in the pre-second world war era, roughly speaking, the banking network was wont to await a creative solution (i.e., a technological shift), snap it up when it was somewhat past its pioneering phase, and then proceed to foment the boom, thereby flooding the markets with 'money' by means of credit.[2] Businesses were allotted credit lines, and by drafting cheques on such accounts, they could wrest resources away from their former employment by bidding up their prices. This was the typical inflationary ignition of the boom.

In time, market saturation, misalignment of economic fundamentals and gradual insolvency all contributed to narrow profitable spreads. Prices plummeted, and so did business earnings: the rate of profit would descend dangerously close to the bank rate. At last, interest would overtake the rate upon capital (profitability), and the system would be finally immobilised: the *deflationary* slump settled upon the markets – the rate of return of businesses had sunk below the bank rate. Banks shut off the spigots. 'Money is tight,' so the crowds would then say. And while unemployment rose, those business concerns that had 'cashed in' before the storm (generally the large financial institutions and, nowadays, private-equity concerns), would proceed to scavenge from the distressed economy deeds, shares, bonds, and real estate at slashed prices, and thereby tilt a highly concentrated distribution of wealth further in their favour. After the rummaging, they would wait. They waited for the next boom, when a 'new technological paradigm' would be just around the corner. The property they had amassed would form the basis (the so-called collateral, or security) for the next expansion of credit. What, then, is a most unnatural husbanding of the economic organism – its stimulation by spasms – has been up to this day construed as an inalterable fact of life by the ordinary person subjected for millennia to a traditional regime of imperishable money – immutable like the scansion of the seasons. The so-called 'business cycle' has now become a mainstay of western folklore.

2. Bretton Woods

Since the second war this system has remained virtually the same, though it was modified in one significant aspect. The potential for *deflation* – the chronic malady of the 1930s characterised by the simultaneous manifestation of declining prices, growing unemployment and income contraction – was reversed by a policy of steady inflationary pressure, built into the system by the provisions of the Bretton Woods Conference of July 1944. As known, the new world standard of the *Pax Americana* was a gold-dollar-exchange anchored on the promise to redeem the greenback at $35 per fine ounce of gold. The United States went on to inflate massively the money supply providing 1) the international means of payment, and banking *reserves*, to their newly-annexed western satellites – money which these could spend on 2) America's market, the largest in the world.

During post-war reconstruction, the United States accumulated significant trade surpluses vis-à-vis the rest of the world. These surpluses, however, were systematically exceeded by substantial flows of US economic and military investment overseas, which consolidated American hegemony by way of industrial and financial acquisitions. Conventionally stated, America printed dollars and bought the world.

So long as there existed a 'dollar shortage' – i.e. a commercial dependence on US exports, which manifested itself through a strong demand for the American currency – such capital outflows were sustainable: in other words, they did not foment an immediately detectable bout of inflation. But as soon as the european countries had achieved reconstruction and an industrial (exporting) capability of their own, they found their reserves to be such that the 'dollar gap' was finally being closed. This occurred in 1958. America's outgoing dollar flows, however, kept increasing dramatically throughout the 1960s, and its persistent trade surpluses offered little offsetting relief against this steady transfer of dollars earmarked for strategic placement.

It so happened that the central banks of the recipient countries found themselves flooded with dollar balances (presented to them by resident businesses and private citizens) against which they had to issue the equivalent value expressed in the domestic currency. The tricky dimension to this business was that such capitals denominated in dollars thus surrendered by European payees to their central banks, were eventually re-placed ('invested') by the latter in the American market itself. Therefore, America perpetrated two economic injustices at once. First, owing to its hegemonic position, the United States fuelled a ceaseless generation of world *inflation*, as funds earmarked for foreign investment originally issued by the Federal Reserve found themselves *duplicated*: once as converted balances in Europe and twice as capital disposable anew on Wall Street. Second, the dollar, as the currency vested with the role of internationally recognised reserve, permitted the United States the luxury to score chronic capital account deficits,[3] by which it managed, in fact, to 'expropriate' – as French president Charles de Gaulle polemically put it – key industrial assets in Europe, paid for with freely-printed dollars. De Gaulle's economic advisor, Jacques Rueff, referred to the dollar's bullying privilege as that 'marvelous secret of the tearless deficit' (*le déficit sans pleurs*).[4]

From America's viewpoint, however, the adherence to a tempered gold regime entailed an annoying constraint, namely, that creditor countries could actually squeeze a tear or two from the US giant by demanding sooner or later the redemption of their dollar gluts in gold. This, they eventually did. Chronologically, the point at which America's debts to foreign central banks exceeded the value of the US Treasury's gold stock was reached in 1964, 'by which time the US payments stemmed entirely from foreign military spending, mainly for the Vietnam War.'[5] In 1967, France finally resolved to spearhead a run on the dollar by demanding conversion of dollar balances into gold; in March 1968, as President Johnson avowed failure in Vietnam by announcing his withdrawal from American politics, the US gold stock had been so depleted that American strategists awoke to the reality, lamenting bitterly how european financiers had 'forced peace' upon them and caused, indeed, an American president to be ousted.[6]

3. The US Treasury-Bill Standard

Irksome though this was to America, the constructive lesson was quickly learnt by its stewards, who wrought yet another momentous modification on the modern capitalist engine with a view, of course, always to maintain hegemonic control. It was done in 1971, under Nixon. The alteration was straightforward: sever the link to gold (i.e., suspend gold payments), and upgrade to a full-fledged *US Treasury Bill Standard*[7] which, with the addition of further refinements, is the regime under which the world economy has been operating to this day. It was a critical transition – the end of Bretton Woods. The scheme has been deemed Machiavellian in that it cleverly shifted the burden of US external deficits squarely and definitively onto the creditor countries by raising the spectre of dramatic dollar devaluation (Nixon had already driven down the dollar by 30% in the aftermath of the 1971 break). In other words, europeans would be forced to continue to absorb dollars for fear 1) of suffering crippling losses on their dollar reserves, and 2) of seeing their exports to the United States irremediably undercut by protectionism and rival American merchandise boosted by a low dollar. One by one the western allies, including France, fell back into line.[8]

Though America in the early 1970s won the battle with the repudiation of the gold clause, the new post-1971 standard was nonetheless a child of crisis. Thenceforth it was understood that the United States and its satellites, barring a modicum of mercantile wrangling, would have to coordinate monetary policy, for they were in the same boat (America's). However, it was also the case that *both* partners were beginning to suffer acutely from the effects of the 'long downturn' brought about by a general overcapacity of the industrialised world, which was marked by an unambiguous *decline in the manufacturing rate of profit* for the west as a whole. The passage from boom to stagnation was consummated between 1965 and 1973.[9] To compound difficulties for the US administration, the policy of low dollar/cheap US exports as a tool of blackmail became blunted by the end of the 1970s. What had come to weigh against American economic fitness was the unrelenting deterioration of its manufacturing sector – above all the machine-tool industry, which had been the heart of the high-productivity gains spurred by 'Yankee know-how' since the Colbertist policies of American nationalist Alexander Hamilton in 1791. In its stead, American strategists appeared to have pursued 'Pentagon capitalism,' that is, the staging of progressive deindustrialisation to be survived by grain suppliers,[10] on the one hand, and, on the other, clusters of high-tech, high-cost military contractors assigned to realising the projects of the Department of Defense.[11] American productivity began to fall dismally after 1965, and no better indicator of such disarray could be cited than the unravelling of America's automobile production. By 1977 US workmanship was no longer a synonym for quality; for that year and the following, the United Stated registered large trade deficits on its trade balance.[12]

The Nixon administration's policy of deliberate depreciation of the dollar and increased government expenditure to sustain employment and consumption in the midst of stagnation – both requiring the Federal Reserve to pump money ceaselessly – had become toothless by the time they were relayed to President Carter's executive. Because America was, industrially speaking, no longer menacing, not only did the insistent devaluation of the dollar fail to bring relief to the trade balance, but, most importantly, *it actually spurred a massive outflow of capital out of the United States.*[13] Meanwhile, saddled with deepening trade and budget deficits, and fugitive capital to boot, *inflation in America consequently shot into the double digits.* With Carter, the first act of the US Treasury-Bill Standard led to a dead end, prodding the minds of American strategists to reinvent it anew, this time as the formidable globalised, finance-driven 'New Economy' in which we presently toil.

4. Neo-Liberal Coup

1979-81 was the watershed biennium: Paul Volcker,[14] one of Nixon's erstwhile architects of the post-1971 standard, was appointed Chairman of the Federal Reserve to engineer the preliminary phase to 'a major process of self-transformation.'[15] The pervasiveness and intensity of the manoeuvre jointly orchestrated by the directorates of the Fed and of the Reagan executive were such that certain scholars have not shied away from calling it a 'coup'. This was the coup that brought forth the so-called 'Neo-Liberal revolution.'[16] In essence, neo-liberalism's institutional transformation issued from the imperative of seeing foreign capital hitched to the US locomotive. How was it a tale of revolution?

The neo-liberal turnaround was denoted by: 1) a nearly-complete dereliction of manufacturing workmanship in favour of 2) a service economy fronted by finance; 3) a reconfiguration of the capitalist engine, whose combustion was thenceforth made chiefly reliant on speculative froth (bubble dynamics); 4) the repression of prices (inflation) and wages; 5) the imposition of high *real* rates of interest;[17] 6) continuing deficits on the trade balance *and* the government's budget; 7) the 'global' (i.e., imperial) suction of foreign,[18] especially Far Eastern, manufactured commodities unto America's marketplace; 8) an unrestrained and overwhelming resort on the part of the median household to personal indebtedness in order to sustain consumption; and 9) as a result, the adamant reinforcement of a plutocratic, bond-holding elite, whose wealth presently displays patterns of concentration not unlike those of a Banana Republic.

The plan, which has undergone its vicissitudes in the past quarter of a century, has not been wanting in sophistication and suppleness. Let us see why by turning to the headings listed above.

Services: because the 1970s had proven that a generalised state of competitive stalemate – caused by saturation, capacity surfeit, and cheapness from the Far East – could not be overcome, the United States went ahead and virtually sacrificed manufacturing by boosting services instead – finance, above all – as these could be made immune from international competition.[19]

Inflation: this was the chief catalyst of the operation. In the 1970s, inflation had seriously eroded the elite's bonds and stocks, which had suffered negative returns. It was time to 'apologize' to the bondholding class and redress the situation.[20] Between September 1979 and April 1980, Volcker curtailed money growth and progressively escalated the Federal Reserve's short term interest rate, which sent banking's prime over that time period from 12 to 20 per cent.[21] Therefore, 'banking entered its most profitable era since World War II.'[22] In the process, the dollar rapidly appreciated, while the unemployment level reached levels unseen since the Great Depression: officially, 10.8 per cent by the end of 1982. Next, Volcker tackled wages: in order to erase the pressure of labour remuneration upon prices, and to arrange the preconditions for a leveraged bubble economy directed by the shareholding class, plants were re-located either to the South or overseas, legislation was drafted to break union power (beginning with the Democrat administration of Jimmy Carter), and the wealthy were significantly unburdened of tax duties (in 1981, under Reagan).[23] The last thrust, which set the anti-inflation mechanism in full swing, came in 1982 with the steady provision of private credit (or debt). As a consequence, the wealthiest households deriving income from financial assets experienced an explosive surge to more than 14 per cent of national income: an increase of 67 per cent just for the first three years of the coup, 1979-82.[24] Median and low-income families, conversely, embarked on a journey of ever-growing personal indebtedness and gradual loss of economic status. If one looks at the data, the trend underscoring the late stock market excess of the

American economy takes off unambiguously and markedly, not in 1994-95[25] but in 1982[26] – this was all Volcker's groundwork, which his successor at the Fed, Alan Greenspan, successively nurtured for the length of nearly twenty years.[27]

Trade deficits: contrary to the misleading alarms of the press, America has no fear of external deficits; it actually thrives on them. Since the neo-liberal break, US economic ministries set out to target the amount of foreign capital the American economy may attract, and then proceed *on that basis* to accumulate a corresponding trade deficit. Therefore, it isn't true that the United States has been engulfed in a haze of (importing) profligacy, which may only be condoned by parsimonious partners (mostly Asian) willing to extend credit for this putative fit of irresponsible consumerism.

By managing first to strengthen the dollar and second to sustain the level of *real* interest to the historically high mark of 5.8 % throughout the period 1982-1990,[28] the Federal Reserve succeeded, in fact, in re-attracting foreign investment, which allowed the procurement of (excess) imports: America overcame inflation in 1984 and managed, yet again, to run external (this time, trade rather than financial) deficits without tears. Furthermore, this achievement confirmed and dovetailed with the strategic realisation that 'perennial trade deficits are a substitute for high rates of inflation. [For], in essence, an abundant foreign supply of goods and services weakens the domestic pricing power of producers and suppliers. This device can work only if foreigners are prepared to accept claims on assets in exchange for their goods and services.'[29] This is precisely what Volcker's high-rate, high-dollar, inflation-busting policy was designed to accomplish. Yet there was one more crucial gain scored from this web of nested objectives.

Budget deficits: The beauty of the neo-liberal putsch – as understood by another outraged French president, François Mitterrand – was that, by using a policy of high interest rates, the United States could 'siphon savings out of the other industrialized countries to pay for the huge federal deficit that should be paid for by [...] US taxpayers.'[30] Of course, Mitterrand failed to remark that the Europeans, as well as the easterners (especially the Japanese),[31] were glad then, as they have been ever since, to 'invest' in America, owing to the chronic overhang of industrial overcapacity at home, which is always prone to threaten the delicate capitalizations of modern corporations (as discussed above – under the head of 'business enterprise' – in classic Veblenian terms). It is nonetheless true and revealing that, by virtue of having posited itself as the first and unavoidable market of the world, the United States has given itself one more degree of freedom in running continuous federal deficits with a view to pursuing an aggressively statal acquisition and development of hi-tech solutions, mostly for its military industry.[32]

Thus, the neo-liberal revolution has delivered an updated version of the classic circuit of 'imperial levying,'[33] by which, first of all, high interest rates prompt foreign investment; part of the money thus attracted is spent on excess (manufactured) imports, while the Fed keeps printing dollars to continue the strategic policy of foreign investment abroad. In turn, these dollars are bought by foreign central banks from their domestic holders, and subsequently 'invested' in America's debt instruments – mostly US Treasury bills – in order to prevent a steep appreciation of the foreign currency vis-à-vis the dollar.[34] Since Reagan, however, the budget deficit has no longer been incurred to stimulate demand, as in the 1970s, but to perform as a supply-booster,[35] behoving, for the most part, the defence contractors. The novelty in this arrangement was the reliance on foreign capital inflows (financial account in surplus) to shoulder *both* trade and federal deficits, *with the complementary objective of phasing out inflation*: by re-attracting foreign funds to America, Volcker's high-interest rate/strong-dollar switchback 'made it unnecessary for the Federal to monetize the debt' (i.e., to print money with a view to absorbing whatever chunk of public debt American taxpayers and investors would not cover).[36]

So, since the 'coup,' what drives America's external deficit – and hegemonic preoccupation – is the international financial account.[37] Considering moreover that the dollar's supremacy is guaranteed by 1) its being still the chief reserve currency of the central banking system on a global scale (today, foreign central banks presently hold approximately 45 per cent of all outstanding US debt certificates), 2) its invoicing of world trade, and 3) its invoicing of all essential staples (oil, above all),[38] America's powers of economic pressure on Europe and the rest of the world remain as daunting as they've ever been.

To recapitulate: Neo-liberalism has become coterminous with a new debt system that has rescinded most forms of labour protection, and entrusted accordingly the monetary requirements of a majority of ever more impecunious households to the (private) mortgaging interests of a bond-holding class sheltered by tax gains and other regressive legal dispositions (i.e., the rich 'microfinance' the poor and not-so-poor through the intermediation of the credit industry).

Meanwhile, a stable, strong dollar, coupled with high (real) rates of interest, has been found to be the inescapable bait for luring external funds, which will 1) feed the system (imports, federal deficit and military expenditures), and, most importantly, 2) fuel America's 'growth engine' by preferential means of speculative dynamics. So, in the end, the world at large nurtures financial bubbles on Wall Street so that it may export (mainly manufactures) to the United States, while the latter devotes a significant portion of its commercial seignorage, so to speak, to the acquisition of martial know-how that'll keep the trading vassals in line. Imperially speaking, this is an accomplishment.

At this stage, however, one may reasonably wonder whether this circuit does not rest, in fact, upon a fragile equilibrium: in other terms, doesn't the United States have to pay increasingly hefty interest charges on its external debt, which performs such a crucial work of hegemonic regulation? The answer is that it does; yet, again, because of 1) the dollar's privileged status and 2) America's commercial primacy, the United States will show no excessive concern in this regard so long as it manages – as it has so far – *to earn more on its foreign assets than do foreigners on US assets.* The counter-intuitive logic of latter-day empire: here is a world 'debtor,' whose power is such that it is in a position to borrow cheaply and lend dearly.[39]

Epochal though it was, Volcker's regime (1979-1987) suffered from a complex, tortuous and, at times, socially turbulent a history[40] – the sort of chequered, choppy material that, unlike Greenspan's mythology of the 'New Economy,' defies hagiographic treatment. Although inflation had been vanquished in 1984-85 and money markets were buoyant, the ravages inflicted by the soaring dollar upon America's agrarians, beleaguered manufacturers and exporters at large were such that America's chief allies (the G-5) had to be summoned to New York in September 1985 to engineer a decade-long decline of the dollar vis-à-vis the other main currencies – the yen and mark, in particular: this was the so-called Plaza Accord. Thereafter, US interest rates fell vis-à-vis foreign ones, and dollars were sold. The subsequent drop of the dollar calmed the special interest groups momentarily,[41] but, given the fading contribution of US manufacturing to national income, the Plaza meeting obviously failed to bring about the much touted turnaround in the trade balance.[42]

In those days, growth was slow, interest rates remained high and nothing stood in the way of 'a national binge of borrowing,' as Volcker put it.[43] There began an arm-wrestling match between the Fed, which was bent on attenuating as much as possible the dollar's descent – hence bent on defending high interest rates – and the executive, led by Jim Baker's Treasury, which sought to align money rates with slower growth in view of placating the anxieties of an economy still a bit discombobulated by Volcker's shock therapy. As the rates were eventually lowered in 1986, Volcker came out politically diminished from the scuffle: he would soon be replaced by Alan Greenspan (August 1987). Despite Volcker's forebodings, Wall Street cheered, enthused as it was over 'the twin bonuses of lower oil prices and lower interest rates [...]. From 1982 to 1987, the value of Dow Jones stock had inflated by more than 230 per cent. Yet, real economic growth had totalled only 20 per cent.'[44]

5. The serial bubbles of the 'New Economy'

The first (neo-liberal) crisis, which came to be handled by Alan Greenspan – the stock market crash of October 1987 – taught the newly appointed Governor an important lesson in the monetary management of empire. The reasons behind the crash are understood: logically, after the Plaza, Volcker was loath to see interest rates and the currency fall too brusquely, for such a movement would have undermined that flow of foreign capital – presently animating America's debt and stock markets – which he had channelled back to the United States at considerable effort and cost since 1979. By definition, (foreign) investors shun diminishing yields and the risk of exchange rate depreciation.

> US policy makers were caught in a bind, needing relatively low interest rates and a low dollar to spur the manufacturing sector *and the opposite to prop up finance.* This is a conundrum they were never able to solve, and the outcome, sooner rather than later, was the stock market collapse of 1987 [...].[45]

A trillion dollars' worth of nominal wealth was effaced by the shock.[46] Though the loss appeared substantial (before the seizure, the total stock wealth stood at 3.2 trillion dollars), the system hardly appeared to have lost momentum. In the first performance of what would become a regular pattern of rescue operations, Greenspan forthwith lowered the Federal Fund Rate by half a percentage point and created (ex nihilo, as it normally goes) 'the funds' to plug the losses of those brokerages that had found themselves most exposed to the shock.

Chart 1

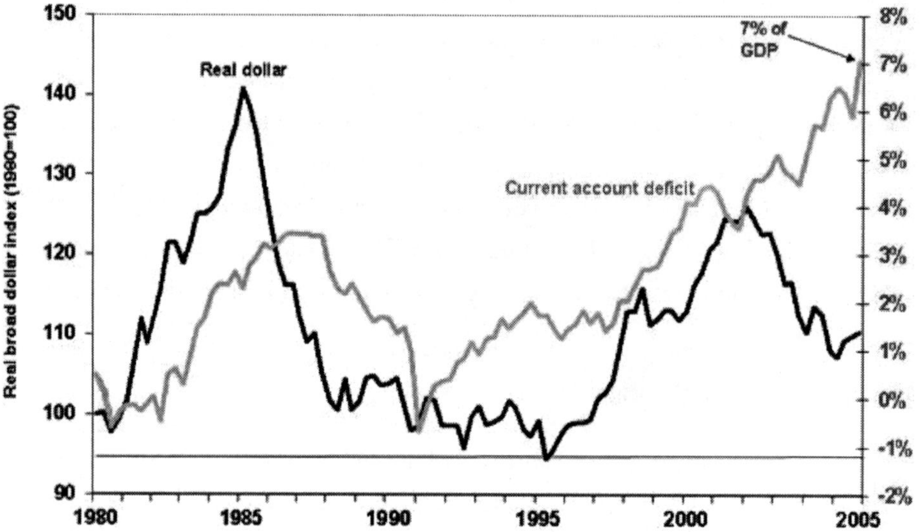

Source: Federal Reserve Board of Governors, Bureau or Economic Analysis and Economic Policy Institute

Chart 2

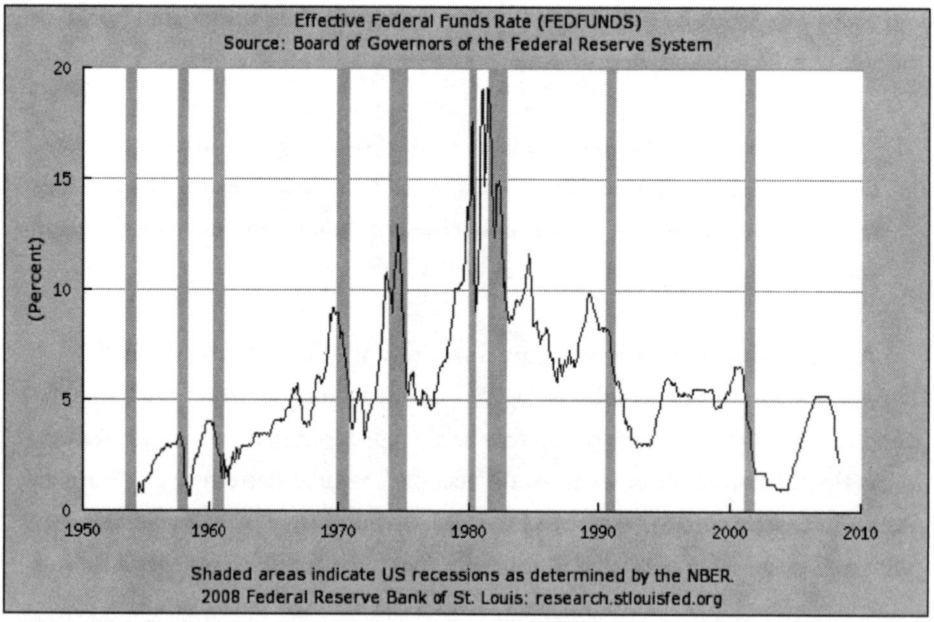

Chart 3

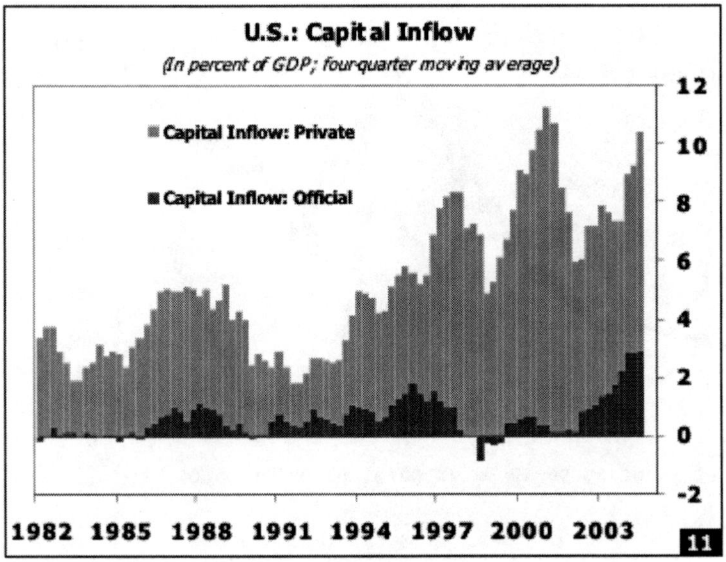

Source: www.imf.org/external/np/speeches/2005/031505.htm

Chart 4

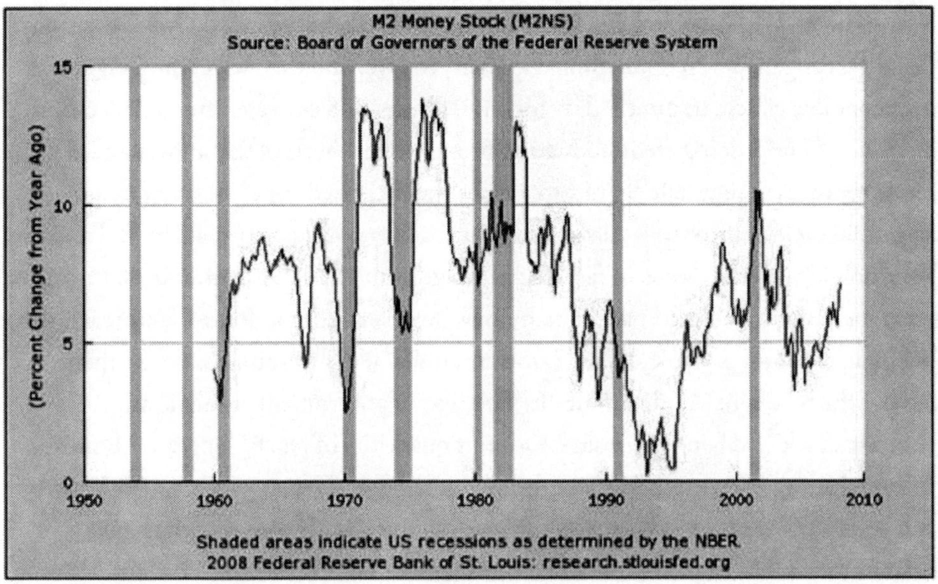

Chart 5

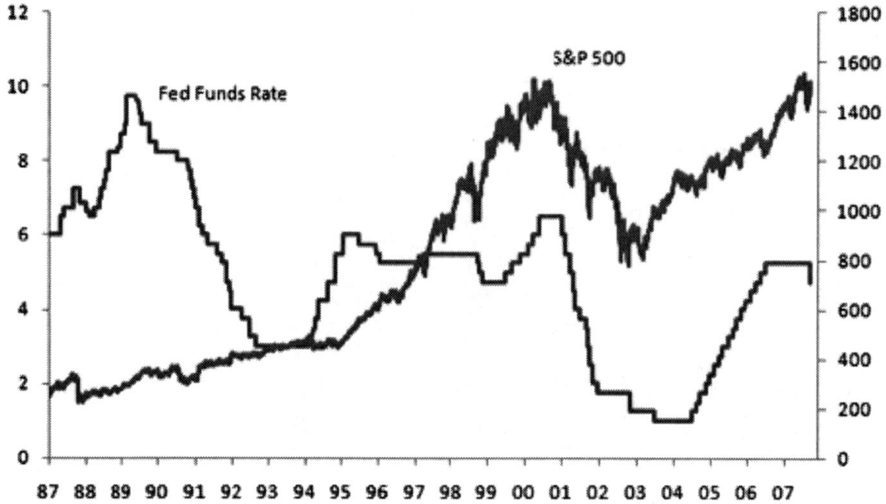

The tug-of-war between Bush Senior's Treasury (this time led by ex-investment banker Tom Brady) and the Federal Reserve was resumed thereafter, as the central bank, given the low level of the post-Plaza dollar, saw no alternative to high rates as the means to shore up foreign investment (see charts 1-5; for relative commentary, refer to notes 37, 52, 55 and 69). If the dollar was weak, as New York Fed Governor, Gerald Corrigan, put it, 'something else [had] to give,' and that 'something' signified the economy, which, trammelled by high rates (around 8 per cent) entered recession in 1990.[47] 'The ensuing credit reduction brought the wheels of the non-financial economy to an abrupt halt.'[48] Automatically, the Fed eased the rates, and foreign investment relented conspicuously. Yet the setback was momentary, as the Fed and the bondholding interests were, in fact, regrouping: from 1990, the central bank began to print money at a sustained pace. The money, however, did not immediately reach the public in the form of bank loans,[49] but went, instead, to refurbish the banks themselves, which bought bonds with it. 'In violation of government regulations,' Greenspan allowed banks 'to hold enormous quantities of [such] long-term bonds without setting aside funds to cover the associated risk. *These appreciated spectacularly as long-term interest rates declined precipitously*, miraculously restoring the banks' balance sheets.'[50] The profits obtained through this 'clandestine bank bailout,' allowed banks 'to write off bad debts and create credit again.' By 1992 the slump was over.[51]

Then came Clinton. Under his presidency, the sum of four key conditions engendered the recent dot.com flare-up, which gave life to the greatest financial bubble in American history (1995-2000). First, as the economy reflated, interest rates were driven up, and the pace of foreign investment took off accordingly (see charts). Second, beginning in January 1993, money creation, magnified by credit extension, rose dramatically.[52] Third, Greenspan talked Clinton into reducing the budget deficit especially through spending cuts,[53] probably to deflect as much foreign funding as possible to the bond and stock markets. And, fourth, as the United States seemed keen on abandoning for good any pretension to manufacturing competitiveness, it proceeded to relieve its commercial partners – Japan and Germany above all – of exchange rate disadvantage by sponsoring in the summer of 1995 the so-called Reverse-Plaza agreement, which implemented the participants' resolution that, once again, the dollar ought to rise against the other main currencies.[54] This last event was of decisive importance.[55]

All of the above traits, coupled with the unflinching commitment to repress wages and extort profits from the service sector by means of exploitative working schedules,[56] yielded the contour of the looming 'New Economy.' Finance triumphant, a high dollar, cheap credit, low pay and the grooming of a bondholding class – whose assigned duty has been to set the spending tone for the country as a whole by leveraging the 'wealth effect'[57] – seemed altogether to re-propose the recipe of Reaganomics, the crucial difference being, however, that the dependence on deficit spending was for the time being almost entirely traded off for speculative hysteria.

Between 1995 and March 2000, when the bubble was officially pricked, stocks on Wall Street had reached vertiginous heights – values, by definition, wholly disconnected from the assets' underlying economic worth. It was said that America's 'growth engine' – i.e., its 'gravity-defying' stock market[58] – had pulled the bandwagon of the world for the whole length of the 1990s, which were accordingly referred to as 'fabulous,' 'wonderful.'[59] The rationale advanced by the establishment (Greenspan's Fed *in primis*) to account for the wonder was a mendacious tale rooted in the claim that, thanks to prodigious advances in hi-tech, US productivity had made extraordinary progress throughout the boom. Hence the stock market appreciation. In truth, the unexceptional technical advances recorded in that decade appeared to be confined to hi-tech manufacturing, which contributes a paltry 4 per cent to US GDP. That such a circumscribed innovation push could justify price-earning ratios of 207 on Wall Street seems unlikely: in December 1999 the stock market was valued at 180 per cent of GDP.[60] Instead, one of the critical realities propelling the stock market boom seems to have been American finance's spectacular sales pitch, whose defining strength, amidst the ballyhoo, *was a sizeable surplus in the total trade balance in advanced technology products.* Interestingly, this balance enjoyed a new spurt during the boom, but immediately thereafter (from 2001 to the present) turned consistently *negative* 'for the first time in recent history.'[61]

When the air was taken out of the bubble, approximately 7.8 trillion dollars' worth of nominal claims was erased. To add travesty to flop, the system had allowed 'the entire US private sector' to enjoy the view at the peak of the gambling[62] euphoria (1996-2000) while it '*was suffering a decline in profitability*.'[63] Indeed, the total profits raked in by the 4200 firms listed at the time on NASDAQ during the five-year bonanza amounted to slightly less than the total losses these self-same concerns registered when the bubble bust: rather than a 'New Economy,' these figures bespoke of a zero-sum heist. All in all, it was reckoned that rising equity prices had accounted for nearly 30 per cent of the increase in GDP during the boom.[64]

Yet none of this truly spoke of calamitous debacle, for in the space of a year and a half, the Fed was at it all over again, priming this time around, *housing*, which had itself begun to inflate along the dot.com boom in 1995 as a by-product of the wealth effect. Despite Greenspan's exhilaratingly disingenuous claims that his agency could not discern the financial outline of a bubble 'until after the fact,'[65] the pattern of short-term interest rates illustrates unambiguously how the Fed monitors and engineers, with ability, these 'soft landings' from the hazardous heights of one bubble to the next. The principle is simple: by ratcheting up interest rates as stock (or housing) quotations increase (charts 5 and 6) the central bank rations credit on one hand, and keeps the bubble within manageable boundaries on the other.[66] Until, that is, the bubble finally pops; then, the skill consists in allowing for the evaporation of trillion dollar losses without stalling altogether the economy, whose price level and unemployment rates are thus sheltered, as best as possible, from the shock on the speculative markets. Thereafter, the short-term rate is forthwith and abruptly lowered to allow for 'restructuring' ('clandestine bank bailouts' and the like), until the system, in traditional fashion, finds itself geared for the next speculative fix.

Chart 6

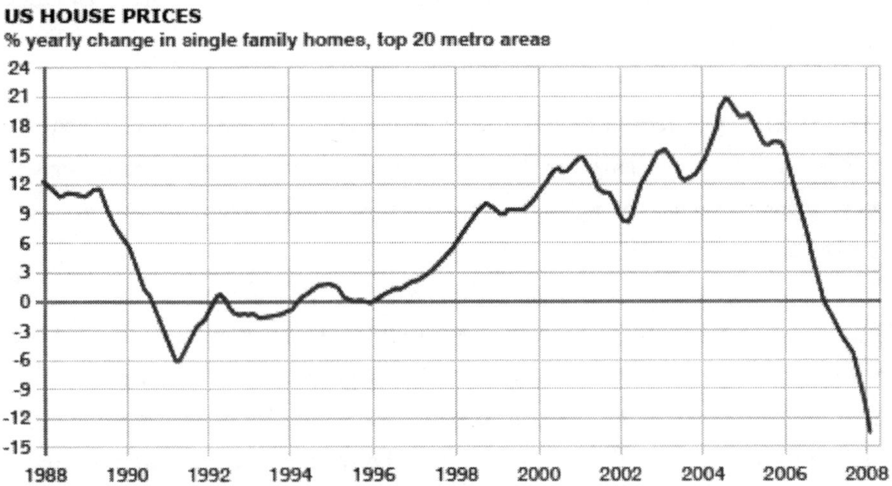

Source: Standard & Poor/Case-Schiller Index

Chart 7

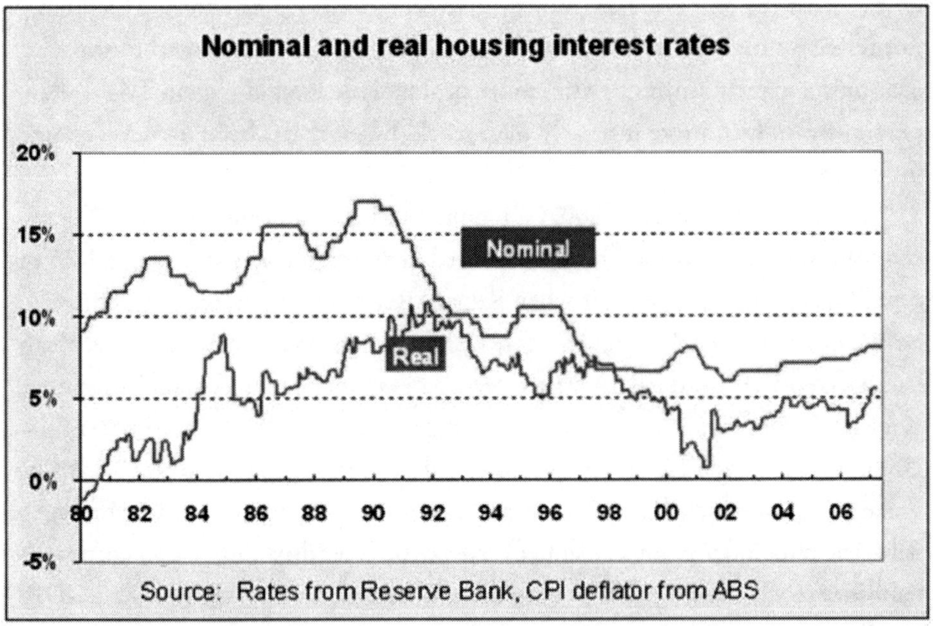

In the last stretch of this 'serial bubble dependency,'[67] housing, as said, became the next target as the real mortgage rate was brought to the historically low mark of 5 per cent (chart 7).

> As long-term rates trended steadily downward in the second half of the 1990s, the big banks plunged headlong into the refinancing, or 'refi,' business. It took a couple of years for consumers to catch on – extracting money from your house was an exotic concept.[68]

When real estate values began to swell in 2002-03, money creation took off accordingly, followed by an upswing in foreign capital inflow and renewed ferment on Wall Street.[69] By the end of 2004, the Federal Reserve tightened again, and in mid-2006 – the terminal point of a second five-year-cycle – this bubble popped as well. We are witnessing the after-effects as we write. Again, the frenetic activity spurred by housing and construction, like the dot.com stocks of yesteryear, appears to have contributed nearly 30 per cent of GDP growth during the cycle,[70] and culminated in a tumble, whose annihilation of virtual wealth is expected in the course of 2009 to run, again, into trillions of dollars.[71] The similarities with the past end here, however, for the late housing excess, which has not relied on high interest rates and a strong dollar, has bequeathed to the economy a greater and somewhat more problematic load of personal debt than previously. In fact, more intensely than stock, housing has been used as collateral for securing credit.

In the fourth quarter of 2007, US household debt amounted to 133.7 per cent of disposable income, and the personal saving rate stood at negative 1.25 per cent.[72] It had been 12 per cent when Ronald Reagan first entered the White house, in 1981: over the span of a generation, America's residual powers of thrift had been entirely disabled. During Greenspan's tenure at the Federal Reserve, 'debt levels rose from $28,898 for the average family in 1987 to $101,386 in 2005.'[73] At the end of 2007, total household debt itself amounted to 13.8 trillion dollars, 10.5 of which (i.e., 76 per cent) was in the form of outstanding mortgage debt, the remainder being consumer credit debt.[74] Adding public and corporate liabilities to this figure yields a cumulative US debt 3¼ times greater than GDP.[75] Finally, in terms of personal indebtedness, the present situation is such that for the median household, the net worth (total assets minus total liabilities ca. $93,000) is roughly twice the annual income, 20 per cent of which is deducted for servicing the debt.[76]

In view of such developments is the system uneasy? Are the markets jittery and the masses simmering? Or is the US executive preoccupied with issues of 'financial sustainability,' or the dreaded 'meltdown'? Hardly. Certainly, the dollar is now (fall/winter 2008) at historical lows – and its plunge since the fourth quarter of 2006 to date, again, may be elegantly accounted for by the drop in foreign capital inflow,[77] which is a forthright consequence of the housing slump. Because of it, the forthcoming upswing, which will possibly herald a boom fuelled by the securitisation of *alternative sources of energy*,[78] is still believed to be 'several years away.'[79]

But, overall, investors trust in Ben Bernanke's Fed, which, they say, by intervening openly in defence of the banking system, is 'in the process of creating a new financial system.'[80] And they harbour no fear of a protracted consumption slump in the midst of foreclosure. Cyclical, opportune write-downs of fictitious wealth à la Greenspan – some call it the 'euthanasia of impaired assets' – should always solve the problem: ultimately, if the price of a house should fall below the value of the mortgage, the financiers' recommendation is for banks to repossess the property while allowing the former owner to remain as a tenant, bound thenceforward simply to remit rent.[81] Thus the conversion of a bad loan into a perpetuity should seal the deal, and onto the next stock market adventure. After all, the bondholders conclude, 'the richest 20% of Americans drive 40% of the country's consumer spending, and their outlays are less restrained by rising gasoline prices and higher mortgage rates.'[82]

Indeed. Since Volcker's coup and Reaganomics, aside from the annulment of households' savings, the millions living below the poverty line have risen from 29 to 36.[83] And suffice it to note that in 2004 the wealthiest 1 per cent of the American population owned 62 per cent of all private business income, 51 per cent of all stocks, and 70 per cent of all bonds.[84]

Undemocratic and spasmodic though it may be, this system is *resilient*. To mitigate its current *défaillances* (especially generalised insolvency and the sudden jump in joblessness), Obama's executive is gearing up to implement a mix of rescue measures: refurbishments of ponderous financial conglomerates by way of freely-printed cash injections (favouring those 'too big to fail'); rescue loans to Detroit's wrecked automakers; allotments of hundreds of billion dollars' worth of public projects; and the promise of additional 'breaks,' such as tax remissions for the middle to low income brackets. 'Bailout' is the magic word these days. Yet, presently, the masses exhibit very little confidence in the face of what appears to them as a slump made to last. Financiers, bankers and the like, on their part, while acknowledging that the road ahead will be rough – they are looking to 2010 for the bounce back – are keen on the other hand to reassure us all that what is going on is by no means the end of the world, and that all we have to await patiently is for the system to 'de-leverage.' Which is to say, in strictly classical fashion, that the financial apparatus quite obviously needs to shed the 'toxic' subprime flotsam and like securitised packages – i.e. the worthless paper acquired by investors/savers late in game (2004-2006) – and begin again. The outer layers of papers are thus being dumped, and the air terminally squeezed out of this last asset-bubble. Meantime banks in the USA are being recapitalised in view of the next scheme, while some folks, besides, are likely to be reintegrated in the medium-term by more or less aggressive (that much remains to be seen) state-sponsored brick and mortar projects. Considering that, for the reasons explicated previously, the world is for the time being chained to America's rattled investment halls, the US administration looks upon the unabashed issuance of bailout money without fear of inflation. If a spurt in the price level is to be expected, however no hyperinflationary collapse of the dollar should be contemplated since all other alternative reserve currencies – against which the dollar would hypothetically suffer this catastrophic depreciation – belong to countries deeply involved in the American game (the European bloc, Japan, and even China).

NOTES

1. *The Economist*, 'Barbarians at the Vault,' May 17th 2008.
2. See Thorstein Veblen's Classic exposition of credit creation in the era of Big Business: *The Theory of Business Enterprise*, New York: Charles Scribner's Sons, 1904, Chapter V, pp. 92-132.
3. Such deficits became inevitable as the receipts of a positive trade balance were greatly and systematically outweighed by outgoing financial flows.
4. Jacques Rueff, *Le péché monétaire de l'occident*, Paris: Plon, 1971, pp. 24, 92.

5. Michael Hudson, *Superimperialism. The Origin and Fundamentals of US World Dominance*. London: Pluto Press, 2002, p.16.
6. Ibid, p. 307.
7. Ibid, p. 17.
8. Ibid, pp. 18, 22, 340, 351.
9. Robert Brenner, *The Boom and the Bubble. The US in the World Economy*, London, New York: Verso, 2002, p. 18.
10. Hudson, *Superimperialism*, p. 28.
11. Seymour Melman, *Profits without Production*. New York: Alfred Knopf, 1983.
12. Thibaut de Saint-Phalle *Trade, Inflation and the Dollar*. New York: Praeger, 1985, p. 291.
13. Ibid, pp. 18, 111-12.
14. Volcker had been Under-Secretary of the Treasury under Nixon, and was serving as Governor of the Federal Reserve Bank of New York at the time of the appointment. Presently, at 81, Volcker heads President Obama's Economic Recovery Advisory Board – a new body within the White House created to oversee the new administration's policies for stabilizing financial markets (see Patrick Martin, 'Who is Paul Volcker? Obama appoints a longtime enemy of the working class,' *World Socialist Web Site*, 28 November 2008, http://www.wsws.org/articles/2008/nov2008/volc-n29.shtml).
15. Robert Brenner, *The Economics of Global Turbulence. The Advanced Capitalist Economies from Long Boom to Downturn, 1945-2005*, London, New York: Verso, 2005, p. 162.
16. Gérard Duménil, and Dominique Lévy, *Capital Resurgent. Roots of the Neoliberal Revolution*. Cambridge, Massachusetts: Harvard University Press, 2000, pp. 9, 14-15.
17. Real interest rates are obtained simply by subtracting a chosen measure of inflation (GDP deflator, Consumer Price Index, Producer Price Index ...) from the nominal rate of interest.
18. Emmanuel Todd, *Après l'empire. Essai sur la décomposition du système américain*. Paris: Gallimard, 2004, p. 109.
19. Brenner, *Global Turbulence*, p. 152.
20. William Greider, *Secrets of the Temple. How the Federal Reserve Runs the Country*. New York: Simon & Schuster, 1987, pp. 167, 552.
21. The data sequence for the prime rate in the eighties runs thus: 1980: 15.3; 1981: 18.9; 1982: 14.9; 1983: 10.8; 1984: 12.4; 1985: 9.9; 1986: 8.3; 1987: 8.2; 1988: 9.3; 1989:

10.8; 1990: 10.0. The series is taken from Kenneth Weiher, *America's Search for Economic Stability. Monetary and Fiscal Policy since 1913*, New York: Twayne Publishers, 1992, p. 174.

22. Greider, *Secrets of the Temple*, p. 411.
23. Brenner, *Global Turbulence*, pp. 211-12, and Greider, op.cit., pp. 430, 451, 542.
24. Greider, op. cit., p. 456.
25. That is, at the time Fed Chairman Alan Greenspan, Volcker's successor, oversaw the dot.com bubble.
26. See Robert Shiller, *Irrational Exuberance*. New York: Broadway Books, 2000, p. 6; Greider, op. cit., p. 705; and Brenner, *The Boom and the Bubble*, p. 100.
27. E. Ray Canterbery, *Wall Street Capitalism. The Theory of the Bondholding Class*. Singapore: World Scientific Press, 2000, p. 48.
28. Brenner, *Global Turbulence*, p. 198.
29. Peter Warburton, *Debt & Delusion. Central Bank Policies That Threaten Economic Disaster*. New York: Allen Lane, The Penguin Press, 1999, p. 27.
30. Quoted in Thibaut de Saint-Phalle, *The Federal Reserve. An Intentional Mystery*. New York: Praeger, 1984, pp. 96-97.
31. Brenner, *The Boom and the Bubble*, p. 54.
32. Michel Ruch, *L'empire attaque. Essai sur le système de domination américain*. Nantes : Éditions Amalthée, 2007, pp. 86 and ff.
33. Todd, *Après l'empire*, pp. 107-11.
34. Anton Brender, and Florence Pisani, *La nouvelle économie américaine*. Paris: Economica, 2004, pp. 136-42.
35. Ibid, p. 102.
36. De Saint-Phalle, *The Federal Reserve*, p. 113; and Greider, *Secrets of the Temple*, p. 561.
37. Of the three main approaches to the US international imbalance, 'the capital flows view,' according to which the trade and current account deficits are a *residual*, the result of the capital account surplus,' is the correct one for reading current events. In other words, the magnitude of America's trade deficits appears to be dictated by the flows of foreign capital, which are themselves determined by the level of interest rates. The other two approaches, focusing respectively on trade and GDP – the former emphasizing how excess imports come first and capital follows to fund the shortfall; and the latter how the trade deficit is the result of a mismatch between domestic savings and domestic investments – fail to account for the

several turning points encountered in the current account's time series (see for instance, Mieczyslaw Karczmar, 'The US Balance of Payments: Widespread Misconceptions and Exaggerated Worries,' *Deutsche Bank Research: Current Issues*, October 1, 2004). As may be evinced from the above charts 1 and 2, the dynamics of interest rate-setting mark the shifts in the current account deficit fairly accurately: for instance, when Volcker tightened the money supply and hiked the FFR (the Federal Funds Rate is the economy's short-term benchmark rate, set by the Federal reserve) in 1979-1982, thus strengthening the dollar and reviving instantly the supply of foreign capital (see chart 3), the current account deficit swelled at once. In the aftermath of the Plaza Accord, as the FFR was brought down to 6 per cent in 1986, the course of the deficit was reversed: it reached a peak in 1987 (3.5 per cent of GDP) – not coincidentally the year of the stock market crash, and gradually settled to a plateau of approximately 1 per cent of GDP by 1990. The maverick datum of 1991, for which year the record shows an exceptional current account *surplus* (of roughly 4 billion dollars) is significant, indeed, for it provides additional proof that capital inflows cause imports, and not vice versa. It came to pass that in that year Bush I launched the war against Iraq. For staging and producing the show, America made its allies pledge 43 billion dollars, which dramatically boosted the net transfer component of the current account, and enabled it to score a slender plus (0.1 per cent of GDP). As news of the pledge was officially broadcast, the *New York Times* revealingly exulted: 'As a result of the war in the Persian Gulf and its aftermath, the United States is likely to borrow far less from abroad this year than last. Many forecasters expect the deficit in the current account – the broadest gauge of the nation's imports of goods and services—to shrink sharply in 1991' (Sylvia Nasar, 'US Trade Benefits from War,' *The New York Times*, March 31, 1991. The *Times'* article mentions, instead, a figure of 51 billion dollars; the sum of 43 billion dollars is taken from Kathryn Morisse, 'US International Transactions in 1991,' *Federal Reserve Bulletin*, May 1992).

38. Ruch, *L'empire attaque*, p. 88.
39. Brender and Pisani, *La nouvelle économie américaine*, pp. 118-19. Earnings accruing from American foreign investment, which are recorded under the Income heading of the Current Account, have been particularly strong for US 'holding companies, led by those holding operating affiliates in computer services and pharmaceuticals,' Christopher L. Bach, 'US International Transactions in 2007,' US Bureau of Economic

Analysis, *Survey of Current Business*, Volume 88, n. 4 (April 2008), http://www.bea.gov/scb/pdf/2008/04%20April/0408_ita-text.pdf.

40. As when the Fed Chairman had to hire a bodyguard to protect himself from popular rage after hitting the economy with prohibitive rates in the early eighties, see Greider, *Secrets of the Temple*, pp. 461 and ff.
41. Over the length of two years – between early 1986 and the end of 1987 – the trade-weighted index of the dollar fell by almost 30 per cent (See *The Economist*, 'Economic Focus: Divine Intervention,' March 27th 2008, p. 100).
42. Yoichi Funabshi, *Managing the Dollar: From the Plaza to the Louvre*. Washington, D.C.: Institute for International Economics, 1988, pp 1, 4, 9, 15.
43. Greider, *Secrets of the Temple*, pp. 657, 679.
44. Ibid, pp. 696, 705.
45. Brenner, *Global turbulence*, p. 277.
46. Steven K. Beckner, *Back From the Brink: The Greenspan Years*. New York: John Wiley & Sons, 1996, p. 62.
47. Beckner, *Back From the Brink*, p. 123.
48. Richard A. Werner, *Princes of the Yen. Japan's Central Bankers and the Transformation of the Economy*. Armonk, NY: M.E. Sharpe, 2003, p. 125.
49. John P. Judd and Bharat Trehan, 'Money, Credit, and M2,' *Federal Reserve of San Francisco Weekly Letter*, Number 92-30, September 4, 1992.
50. Brenner, *Global Turbulence*, p. 278, emphasis added.
51. Werner, *Princes of the Yen*, p. 125.
52. As may be seen from Chart 4, M2 – the broad monetary aggregate comprising currency, deposits and savings – took off in 1993, after Greenspan's 'clandestine bank bailout' was completed during the previous biennium.
53. Beckner, *Back From the Brink*, p. 300.
54. From the last quarter of 1995 to the beginning of 2002, when the dot.com bubble had fully deflated, the real trade-weighted index of the dollar increased approximately by a third (see Chart 1).Brenner, *The Boom and the Bubble*, p. 131, and *Global Turbulence*, p. 290.
55. When the Federal Reserve hiked interest rates at the beginning of 1994 (see Charts 2 and 5), foreign investment, which had been in a lull throughout the recession of the early nineties, picked up again (Chart 3). The dollar's appreciation orchestrated by the Reverse-Plaza Accord of 1995 (Chart 1), along with the Fed's steady injection of

liquidity into the economy (magnified by bank lending; Chart 4), began to fuel the stock market boom (Chart 5), whose stellar yields, in turn, took over from the interest-rate policy the task of attracting further, copious foreign funds. As said, it is from such capital inflow that America recoups its current account (trade) deficit.

56. Ibid, p. 335.
57. That is the stimulation of consumption generated by way of capital gains (paper, virtual earnings), rather than by concrete advancement in labour remuneration.
58. Alan S. Blinder and Janet L. Yellen, *The Fabulous Decade. Macroeconomic Lessons from the 1990s*. New York: The Century Foundation Press, 2001, p. 53.
59. Ibid, p. 1.
60. The work conventionally cited by commentators doubting the story of the New Economy's productivity surge is Robert J. Gordon, 'Does the 'New Economy' Measure up to the Great Inventions of the Past?,' [2000]. *Journal of Economic Perspectives,* Vol. 14, No. 4, Fall, p. 49-74. www.nsf.gov/statistics/seind06/pdf/overview.pdf. Moreover, it shall not be bootless to bear in mind that downright statistical manipulation was effected by conniving governmental statistical bureaus in order to inflate the numbers, in support of the Fed's self-congratulatory fabrications; see William Fleckenstein, *Greenspan's Bubbles. The Age of Ignorance at the Fed.* New York: McGraw Hill, 2008, pp. 117-120.
61. The National Science Board, *Science and Engineering Indicators*, 'Overview,' 2006, pp. 7-8. For specific data, consult: http://www.census.gov/foreign-trade/statistics/country/index.html.
62. Shiller, *Irrational Exuberance*, p. 41.
63. Peter Hartcher, *Bubble Man: Alan Greenspan and the Missing Seven Trillion Dollars.* New York: W. W. Norton & Company, 2006, pp. 9, 13-14.
64. Brenner, *Global Turbulence*, pp. 296, 312.
65. As contended by the Fed Chairman during his testimony in front of the Senate Banking Committee, April 13, 2000.
66. This is the classic monetary phenomenon of the *hausse* – also acknowledged by Gesell – whereby initially low, boom-triggering rates eventually accompany the ascent of the credit inflation, to keep abreast of the nominal price increases. See Silvio Gesell, *The Natural Economic Order, Money Part (Part 1)*, San Antonio: Free-Economy Publishing Co., 1934 [1919], p. 275, and de Saint-Phalle, *The Federal Reserve*, p. 90.
67. Hartcher, *Bubble Man*, p. 24

68. Charles S. Morris, *The Trillion Dollar Meltdown. Easy Money, High Rollers and the Great Crash*. New York: Public Affairs, 2008, p. 67.
69. The trajectory of the Federal Funds Rate (Charts 2 and 5) seems to indicate that the Fed, by July 2004, must have regarded housing prices sufficiently high to require a standard, gradual interest *hausse*, which, as was the case for the dot.com bust, is effected to burst the bubble in 18 months or so.
70. Brenner, *Global Turbulence*, p. 311.
71. Dean Baker, 'The Housing Bubble and the Financial Crisis,' *Real-world Economic Review*, issue no. 46, May 2008. See also, Morris, *Trillion Dollar Meltdown*, pp. 132-33.
72. Board of Governors of the Federal Reserve System, *Monetary Policy Report to the Congress*, 27 February 2008, p. 9. http://www.federalreserve.gov/boarddocs/hh/2008/february/fullreport.pdf.
73. William Bonner, and Addison Wiggin, *Empire of Debt. The Rise of an Epic Financial Crisis*. New York: John Wiley & Sons, 2006, pp. 253, 257.
74. *Flow of Funds of the United States*, March 8, 2008 Release, Z-1 Release, Debt Outstanding Tables, *Federal Reserve Statistical Release*, 6.
75. Fleckenstein, *Greenspan's Bubbles*, see chart on p. 174.
76. See John Bellamy Foster, 'The Household Debt Bubble,' *Monthly Review*, Volume 58, no. 1, May 2006, www.monthlyreview.org/0506jbf.htm; and Kevin L. Kliesen, 'Survey Says Families Are Digging Deeper into Debt,' *The Regional Economist, The Federal Reserve Bank of St. Louis*, July 2006,
77. Board of Governors of the Federal Reserve System, *Monetary Policy Report to the Congress*, 27 February 2008, p. 18.
78. *The Economist*, 'The Future of Energy,' June 21st 2008, p. 17.
79. Eric Martin, 'US Stocks Drop as Oil Climbs; UPS, General Motors Retreat,' *Bloomberg*, July 1st 2008.
80. Randall W. Forsyth, 'Bearing Down on the Fed's Balance Sheet,' *Barron's*, April 4, 2008. When the Federal Reserve recently pioneered the rescue of investment firm Bear Stearns by extending loans to the latter and other involved financial outfits (thus absorbing in exchange their IOUs into its own portfolio, and sacrificing Treasuries as a result), it somehow innovated with respect to Greenspan's routine of merely providing cheap money whenever the system tottered. Some analysts have thought the change so momentous that they have begun discriminating between 'pre-Bear Stearns' and 'post-Bear Stearns' procedures in financial chronicling.

81. Thomas G. Donlan, 'A Change of Status,' *Barron's*, May 26, 2008.
82. Kopin Tan, 'A Bullish Call,' *Barron's*, December 17, 2007.
83. 'In 2003 the Census Bureau defined the poverty line for an individual by an income of $9,573 and for a family of four by an income of $18,660,' Ravi Batra, *Greenspan's Fraud. How Two Decades of His Policies Have Undermined the Global Economy*. New York: Palgrave Macmillan, 2005, p. 227.
84. Morris, *Trillion Dollar Meltdown*, p. 141.

Anarchist Studies 17.1 © 2009 ISSN 0976 3393
www.lwbooks.co.uk/journals/anarchiststudies/

(Tory) anarchy in the UK: the very peculiar practice of tory anarchism

Peter Wilkin

School of Social Science
Brunel University
Uxbridge
UB8 3PH

ABSTRACT

The term 'tory Anarchism' is reasonably well known but largely unanalysed in either popular or academic literature. It describes a group of apparently disparate figures in English popular and political culture whose work has, in part, satirised key British institutions and social relations. At the same time, tory anarchists also provide interesting insights into questions of British, though predominantly English, identity, by focusing upon issues of class, empire and nation. This article examines tory anarchism by focusing upon four representative figures: Evelyn Waugh, George Orwell, Peter Cook and Chris Morris.

Keywords: *Tory anarchism, popular culture, world system, English identity, empire*

INTRODUCTION: THE SOCIAL ORIGINS OF TORY ANARCHISM

Tory anarchism is a term that describes a group of (largely) English writers and artists who span the twentieth century. As a concept it is infrequently referred to and lacks any systematic analysis in either academic or popular literature. It is a predominantly English phenomenon, associated with men, not women, and members of the middle and upper-middle classes in revolt against what they see as the denigration of the core values of England or the idiocies of the ruling establishment. Although often linked with social satire, tory anarchism is much more than this and embraces ideas about the nation, morality, class, culture and patriotism.[1] The argument that I develop in this paper is that tory anarchism emerges against the background of Britain's changing circumstances as a global power. In particular it should be seen in the following context:

- The end of empire and relative decline of the UK (more specifically England) as a political force. In this respect it is both an evocation of and a commentary upon the changing nature of English identity over the course of the twentieth century.
- An ambivalent reaction to modernity and capitalism that invokes a cultural critique sharing many concerns with those of the Frankfurt School:
  1. The death of the individual;
  2. The rise of authoritarianism and totalitarianism;
  3. The subordination of moral to monetary values;
  4. An ambiguous attitude towards both elite and mass popular culture.

However, tory anarchism offers a profoundly different analysis of these problems and ultimately hankers after a different kind of utopia to those of the critical theorists, one rooted in a romanticised past rather than a romanticised future.

What, then, does it mean, to describe someone as being both a tory and an anarchist? On one level the term is clearly paradoxical; conservatism and anarchism are often seen as political opposites and yet in truth there are often striking overlaps in these political philosophies: a concern with the local and the empirical,[2] the concrete reality of everyday lived experience, as opposed to more abstract, universal theorising;[3] and the importance of class in understanding social order. However, the analyses that orthodox anarchists and conservatives offer to explore these issues are radically different. What can be said to characterise the idea of a tory anarchist then? First, it is an individualist creed. There can be no party of tory anarchists as it is an anti-political stance or posture that would make such an idea impossible in practice. There is no institution in which the tory anarchist is housed and nor is it a political badge that simply anyone can wear. The history of tory anarchism suggests that it is restricted in its meaning to members of a particular social class, working in areas of popular culture. To be a tory anarchist in practice means having an audience for your work, to be someone that has made an impact on popular and political culture. Given the rebellious nature of tory anarchism it is difficult to make a case for lay people adopting the mantle with any degree of conviction. Tory anarchists are essentially public figures who use their public image to unsettle, to question and to challenge the failings and contradictions of English society.[4] In the context of tory anarchy in the UK there is a rich lineage of figures that can be referred to from Swift, Milton and Cobbett through to twentieth century journalists such as Richard Ingrams, Auberon Waugh and Michael Wharton.[5] The social conditions and individual qualities that I have described as being necessary aspects of the character of the tory anarchist can no doubt be found elsewhere in the world system. For example, Louis-Ferdinand Céline in France, and Norman Mailer and Dwight MacDonald in the USA, might reasonably be described in this way. However, this article is concerned with tory anarchism as a predominantly *English* phenomenon and with its distinctive national qualities.

The backdrop to the idea of tory anarchism in the twentieth century is the end of empire and the gradual and relative decline of the UK's global hegemony. In turn this raises the question of the relationship of tory anarchism to conservatism as a political ideology. The deepening of capitalism as a global system undermined many of the ideas, beliefs, values and institutions that conservatives have held dear, especially in the UK. Socialism, in any meaningful sense of the term, has also disappeared from mainstream party politics, with most political parties adhering to some variant of neo-liberalism or, to some extent, social democracy.[6] But while the embedding of capitalism into everyday social relations has presented major problems for all political ideologies, as Wallerstein has noted, conservatism has been dealt a particular blow.[7] The party political ideology of traditional conservativism, which Ian Gilmour characterised as a commitment to one nation, a mixed economy and a pragmatic philosophy, has for the moment largely disappeared from the political landscape.[8]

For the tory anarchist these developments are hugely significant, though the relationship to traditional conservative thought is somewhat ambivalent. Tory anarchists are often bohemians and ironists, exploring themes that are not usually associated with orthodox conservatism. The death of conservatism as a political force is an important target for tory anarchist iconoclasm, providing a prime example of the failure of the traditional ruling class to defend and sustain the values and institutions that helped shape modern England against a crude and vulgar materialist (neo) liberal ideology. Tory anarchists are able to combine a defence of values and institutions that they know to be outmoded, if not reactionary and frequently unacceptable (empire, colonialism, racism, a ruling class and fox hunting), with those typically celebrated in English culture and custom (from the pub to tea-drinking, bad cooking and cricket).

In this paper I focus on four well-known tory anarchists: Evelyn Waugh (1903-1966), George Orwell (1903-1950), Peter Cook (1937-1995) and Chris Morris (1965-). Each of these men has used the dominant cultural formats of their time to explore their ideas about Englishness and identity. Waugh, Orwell, and Cook all worked with first-hand knowledge of the British empire and its disintegration. In his work Morris deals with the consequences of a post-empire and post-modern Britain: the apparent loss of faith felt by many in the grand narratives of identity rooted in the nation, class, politics, religion and science. Although my main concern is with satire I also want to bring out other aspects of their work to give full meaning to the idea of the tory anarchist. Thus the paper will examine their ideas regarding the following key themes: empire, class, nation and popular culture.

TORY ANARCHY AS SOCIAL SATIRE: WAUGH, ORWELL, COOK AND MORRIS

What unites the avowedly socialist Orwell with the radically right-wing and racist Evelyn Waugh?[9] What can be said to connect the gregarious public figure of Peter Cook with the intensely private Chris Morris? In short, what is it that gives coherent meaning to the idea of a tory anarchist? There are a number of threads that connect all of these figures. They share a similar social class background, being upper-middle class, public school and university educated.

Waugh came from a middle class family and was one of the 'bright young things' of 1920s England that he went on to satirise in *Vile Bodies*. He was educated at Lancing College and Oxford, where by all accounts he lived a relatively debauched and indulgent life, that of a loafer.[10] However, his relative lack of academic success led him to pursue a variety of jobs that left him deeply unhappy, with a possible attempted suicide by drowning aborted only when he was stung by a jellyfish.[11] Orwell was born in India, where his father worked for the opium department of the civil service. His mother brought him to England when he was one year old and he was subsequently educated at Wellington and Eton.[12] Upon leaving Eton Orwell, as is well known, did indeed choose a career reflecting his social class, joining the Indian Imperial Police, an experience that was to shape his future anti-imperialist politics.[13] Like Orwell, Peter Cook was born into a family where the father was a colonial civil servant. Cook was educated at Radley and Pembroke College, Cambridge where he was perhaps the most famous ever member of the Footlights comedy group. Cook noted in various places that he had been expected to work in the Foreign Office, but his career as a satirist (something he went on to mock with some vehemence) put an end to this possibility.[14] Finally, Chris Morris was educated at Stonyhurst, the Jesuit boy's boarding school in Lancashire, and the University of Bristol.[15] Morris is by far the most private of these figures. His comparatively low public profile has been an important factor in his ability to satirise the media and popular and political culture. The less the media is able to tell us about Morris, the more he is able to retain his cutting edge and autonomy of purpose.[16]

In addition to this shared background, each has a rebellious streak, an aesthetic interest in popular and elite culture, the ability and motivation to take huge risks, the desire to reflect upon, criticise and even profane the very things that they hold most dear. For example, Waugh was both a critic and a member of the bright young things movement; Cook was both a satirist and admirer of Macmillan; Orwell was a democratic socialist who defended provincial English village life and customs, which often entailed bigoted views about homosexuality, foreigners and women; Morris is a master of the modern media age but also a supreme critic of its impact on popular culture. Irony is the cutting edge of the tory anarchist and it is an irony that they are adept at applying to themselves. They are tories in the area of culture; it is a cultural conservatism, not a political one that unites them. They are anarchists in the sense that they are anti-authoritarian, against the state and bureaucratic power, and defenders of individual liberty. In this sense Orwell, the only one of the four who was openly committed politically, is as much a tory anarchist as the other three, though he is without doubt the most problematic figure in the group. Indeed Orwell said of himself that when he was eighteen he was 'both a snob and a revolutionary. I was against all authority';[17] and until 1934, at least, he referred to himself as a 'tory anarchist'.

As with all social practices, satire is rooted in a particular time and place.

Unlike most other forms of English satire, however, tory anarchism knows no bounds in terms of its targets and the extremes of humour to which it will go in order to make its point. As a consequence it provides the most challenging of tests to free speech in its exposure of social folly and vices, whatever the consequences, in the public sphere. There is an irony here in that whilst the idea of the public sphere is most commonly associated with liberal and leftist social thought, in the English cultural mainstream it is the tory anarchist who has arguably pushed the boundaries of free speech and the public sphere the furthest. The work of liberal and leftist satirists is usually situated within part of a broader progressive social movement and has tended to subject itself to self-imposed limits on both its subject matter and the language used – for example, shunning sexist or racist jokes. By contrast, the tory anarchist is the ultimate contrarian, raising issues that others don't and often rubbing the noses of their fellow citizens in the most hypocritical and repulsive aspects of popular and political culture. Evelyn Waugh's treatment of English racism in his early novels; Orwell's satirical attacks on totalitarianism; Peter Cook's then-scandalous impersonation of then Prime Minister Harold Macmillan and the extreme scatology of his fictitious persona in 'Derek and Clive'; and Chris Morris's television programme *Brass Eye* on paedophilia – are all examples, all provoking hysterical reactions from the popular press and politicians.

AGAINST MODERNITY? TORY ANARCHISM AS CULTURAL CRITICISM

The relationship between tory anarchism and modernity is a complex one. Often it takes the form of scathing hostility: Waugh's complaint, articulated in the guise of Gilbert Penfold, that the evils of modern life could be summed up as 'plastics, Picasso, sunbathing and Jazz' is a neat summation of this mood.[18] More tellingly, his novel *The Loved One: An Anglo-American Tragedy* is upon first reading both a shock and a thrill in its characterisation of the vapid and amoral social relations of 1940s Los Angeles. With its exiled English poet Denis Barlow as anti-hero taking advantage of the naiveté and vulgarity of his American hosts whilst working at the garish pet cemetery (the perfectly named 'Whispering Glades'), *The Loved One* is a thoroughly modern novel in style, target, tone and humour. It is written with a dead-pan and vicious wit that enables Waugh to skewer the narcissism and emptiness of modern consumer society. Its relevance for an understanding of the dangers of commodification on social and moral norms has only grown over time. The theme that emerges here and throughout tory anarchist writings is that of human imperfection, the willingness of people to carry out the most awful and often inhumane actions and even to find black humour and pleasure in them. Orwell noted this tendency in his writings on the appeal of fascism, for example.[19] More benignly, tory anarchists find humour in the imperfection and imperfectability of human nature, leading them to dwell upon the often absurd nature of life.[20]

Peter Cook both loved and ridiculed aspects of the modern world. He claimed to spend most of his time reading newspapers, watching television, consuming pornography, listening to rock music and engaging in gossip.[21] His flawed film *The Rise of Michael Rimmer* was a failed attempt to examine and ridicule the rise of public relations in political life as a mechanism for controlling public opinion.[22] As is now well recognised, his theme has become central to political culture in most countries. George Orwell saw the dark aspects of modernity most famously in *1984* where the mass media has become the mechanism of social control and totalitarianism, but he drew upon his experiences at the BBC for inspiration for the idea.[23] Similarly, Chris Morris is accused by his critics of being a symptom of the very decline he satirises, someone who panders to the audience's worst taste. What can be concluded, then, is that tory anarchists have contrary views about the nature of modernity, and in the following section I will examine the major themes in their work to draw out further this contradictory nature.

EMPIRE, CLASS AND NATION: THE END OF ENGLAND?

A major theme of tory anarchist writing has been the apparent erosion and transformation of English identity over the course of the twentieth century. This change in national identity takes place against and within the backdrop of three developments: the end of empire, ruling class weakness and the transformation of the nation and its values.[24]

The end of empire

This theme is addressed explicitly by Waugh, Orwell and Cook, and serves as a cultural backdrop to the work of Chris Morris. Orwell had mixed feelings about empire but ultimately reached a consistent anti-imperialist politics. Empire was a source for some of the works of literature that he most admired, notably Kipling. Equally, it was the source of a general racism in the English ruling classes that he came to despise. The brutality of empire and its deadening effect on the moral consciousness of rulers and ruled alike is explored in the essays 'A Hanging' and 'Shooting an Elephant', and in his accounts of life in the Imperial Police, where Orwell acknowledges with customary honesty that the institution was changing him and moulding him to its own racist norms and values.[25]

For Waugh empire is less problematic but equally indicative of the corrupting effect of power and the decline of England. In both *Scoop* and *Black Mischief* Waugh is able to expose the follies of arrogant ruling class megalomaniacs such as Lord Copper of *The Daily Beast* and Lord Zinc of *The Daily Brute*, in a way that is devastatingly funny, affectionate yet brutally clear about the unaccountable power of media and political elites. Both novels are laced with acerbic observations about the intricate relationship between British racism and the empire, reflected in the complacent and arrogant practices of a ruling class that is increasingly unable to rule with any authority. Infusing his conservatism with Catholicism, Waugh reacted to what he saw as the moral collapse of the world around him and armed himself with the weapons that he needed to express his hatred and intolerance of an atheistic and nihilistic age.[26] The latter themes connect his writing to the work of Orwell and Morris. The former addressed recurrently the question of how to be a good person in a world without faith and Morris likewise focuses upon aspects of Britain's moral and intellectual decline.

By the 1950s the British empire was in full retreat but in ideological terms it continued (and still does) to hold a massive significance in popular and political culture. British politicians continued to act as though they possessed imperial power, as Anthony Eden showed with the attack on Suez in 1956, and as more recently Tony Blair indicated in the offensives against Afghanistan and Iraq. This arrogance and the continued belief in the right to exercise imperial power left Britain's ruling classes of the period open to the attacks of a younger generation who came of age after the Second World War. At the forefront was Peter Cook. Cook's club, 'The Establishment', was the first and most important comedy club in Britain, providing a new generation of satirists with space to vent their spleen against an establishment from which many of them were actually drawn.[27] For

Cook and his peers, the 1950s were not only a period of cultural stagnation and decline but were marked by a series of social conventions that had their roots in Victorian Britain, and seemed increasingly irrelevant to contemporary needs and desires.[28] Cook's aims were to ridicule the manners and morals of an elite that appeared ridiculous in their pretence of imperial power. Cook's work was filled with characters that he would develop later in his career: jaded, violent and corrupt judges, pompous and deluded politicians, the sexually repressed middle classes, stiff-upper-lipped and desperate military officers and perverse public school teachers. In short he was mocking the weaknesses and failures of a generation shaped by empire and its decline.[29]

Class rule

Class is a central concept in the tory anarchist's lexicon and reflects their general ambivalence towards modernity. In practice, classes are sources of rich cultural heritage, humour and values, setting out clear social roles and forms of authority, obligation and morality. Class relations are not vehicles for the analysis of social conflict or revolutionary change. Tory anarchists are committed to a more moral idea: no class is necessarily good or bad in its cultural influence, except the commercial philistines who emerged with modern capitalism.[30] There is a sense of a natural order to the tory anarchist view, which has its roots in English (perhaps British) culture; and an idea of an order that has been fundamentally subverted by modernity and the rise of capitalist society.[31] Under capitalism, the working classes have been transformed into wage slaves and the traditional aristocracy are frequently reduced into a faded and ridiculous grandeur. It is the newly emerging Victorian middle class entrepreneurs with their depressing utilitarian and philistine ethos that has served to destroy the real meaning of English culture: life and liberty. In the *Brass Eye* episode 'Decline', Chris Morris focuses upon the moral decay of Britain, a theme that also predominates in Waugh's work. Morris paints an exaggerated and satirical portrait of a morally decayed and corrupted society that has succumbed to the quintessence of capitalist culture: consumer commodification. At one point he uncovers a map of the UK to reveal that it has lost all 'decency', a theme that resonates in the work of Orwell, too, and which is at the heart of the tory anarchist critique of class: values and manners lost, in a world corrupted by money and profit.

For Waugh the lesson is that the aristocracy and the upper classes remain an important source of inspiration in English culture, notwithstanding their debauchery, stupidity and abnegation of responsibility.[32] Happiness and a good society are to be found in the complex interplay of social classes and the diversity of character and outlook to be found within the nation. The enemy for the tory anarchist is grey uniformity, the homogeneity of class and character that results in societies engineered by the state through social policy. Orwell's concern about the transformative power of the state emerges in his celebrations of the lives of the English working classes, his vivid pictures of the sights, sounds, smells and feel of class as a lived cultural experience, and his worry that western democracies were as vulnerable as the states in the Soviet bloc to the totalitarian pressures of modern bureaucracy.[33]

Rather than the gritty realism of Orwell, Peter Cook inherited the mantle of the aristocratic dandy (shades of Oscar Wilde and Noel Coward perhaps): a brilliant and savage wit who mocks and celebrates the rich array of crazed and crackpot characters that the ruling elite throws up.[34] In 1986, when Cook attacked the ultimate symbol of utilitarian and philistine values – prime minister Margaret Thatcher – he readopted the guise of Harold Macmillan. Whatever Cook's critique of the generation that Macmillan represented, he realised that the former prime minister was as aghast as he was at Margaret Thatcher's philistinism.[35] If Macmillan represented a ruling class at the fag-end of empire, Thatcher was the culmination of everything horrible in the new commercial conservatism.[36]

One nation in decline

The nation is fundamental to conservative politics in general, and for tory anarchists serves as a source of inspiration, meaning, black humour and ultimately satire.[37] In terms of the tory anarchists' vision of a good society (and I make that claim tentatively), the nation is the repository of practices and traditions from which a modern society can and should draw.[38] The history of the nation, particularly its rural past and present, is a site of inspiration for tory anarchism rather than simply being the home of 'rural idiocy', as Marx once described it. It should be stressed, however, that for tory anarchists, the countryside is *also* the home of 'rural idiocy' and therefore a site rich in potential for caricature and humour. For example, Waugh famously adopted the guise of the traditional English country gentleman as part of his transformation into a curmudgeon but admitted he had not the slightest interest in rural life.[39]

Unlike socialist utopians, who imagine a future good society, tory anarchists draw from the qualities of the nation's past for their inspiration. Their view is that English national identity is rooted in a defence of 'life and liberty', a love of play, community and self-help and autonomy. It is an expression of the lived experience and history of a group of people, not a commitment to abstract principles or citizenship or belonging. In undermining these features of national life, modern industrial capitalism has replaced skilled or semi-skilled communitarians with atomised, routinised and de-skilled drones of progress.[40] Life and liberty have been sacrificed for the promise of 'security' in all its forms.

A love of the nation, despite its flaws and often ugly or horrendous past, is a connecting feature of these writers, but in Orwell it perhaps finds its clearest expression. His defence of patriotism in his 'Notes on Nationalism'[41] argued that love of country was a fundamental social and political virtue and something generally lacking in the political left wing. Indeed, Orwell was equally scathing about the mindless 'John Bull' patriotism of the right and the snobbery and intellectual detachment of many leading British socialists, finding that they had nothing in common with the working classes they aspired to represent.[42] Orwell was self-critical about his own relationship to British working class life, but unlike many of his contemporaries could openly admit this.[43] He took his concern with the nation and its culture to focus upon the peculiarities of the English – their love of pubs, vulgar seaside postcards and music-hall humour, even the correct method for making a cup of tea.

It is worth noting that there is nothing sentimental about the tory anarchist view of English culture. On the contrary, the assessments are of its resilience and its contradictory nature: it is the diversity and peculiarity that national identity generates that is so attractive to tory anarchists. For Chris Morris, writing in what I described earlier as a post-modern, multicultural England (what John Gray has described as post-traditional England[44]), a key question emerges here. What happens when a people that was once held together through grand narratives of class, nation and empire begins to reject or move away from those meanings? What does it mean to live in an increasingly multicultural England for the tory anarchist? Morris is ambiguous about this in his work, and I suspect this is because he is unsure about the answers. Rather, he raises awkward questions, pricking the pompous (like Waugh before him) and exposing contradictions, as tory anarchists are wont to do. What is transparent is his mockery of a dumbed-down England of mass culture, moral decline, popular idiocy and shallow intellectual depths, as personified in the rise of a facile celebrity culture.[45] What are the consequences of this for the tory anarchist?

POPULAR CULTURE IN THEORY AND PRACTICE – PROFANING THE PUBLIC SPHERE

In theory – how very un-British

What can tory anarchists tell us about the nature of British popular culture over the course of the twentieth century? It would be an exaggeration to say that tory anarchism represents a coherent social theory, and no doubt its practitioners would regard this suggestion with some mockery and scepticism. At best it is a stance or a position that is taken against the grain of contemporary culture and politics. Nonetheless it is not unreasonable to say that there are certain themes that underlie the position of the tory anarchist, and that at its heart is a moral response– though not a didactic or moralising one – to what is seen as decline in British life, art and culture.

For Waugh the concern is with the defence of the values of true or great art against mere populism. There are echoes of this in the work of Orwell, Cook and Morris, but in general they take a more complicated view of popular culture. Their work exposes the ways in which mass culture in the hands of an oligarchy of media professionals can be used as a mechanism to exploit and corrupt taste, playing on popular fear, ignorance and gullibility.[46]

It is clear that for all of these figures, except perhaps Morris, there was a resistance to theory and theorising, often coupled with a deep hostility to what was seen as unnecessary pretentiousness. Waugh is an ambiguous figure here, in that he experimented with and was influenced by modernist literary style and devices, such as collage, the interior monologue, classical parody, the intrusive narrator, the camera eye, montage. Allen suggests, however, that Waugh's heart was never really in this, and that he used these techniques at least as much as a way of shocking his elders and the public, as through any intellectual commitment to the tradition.[47] In particular Waugh rejected the way in which modernism connected aesthetics and politics in support of wider political projects, something he saw as demeaning and potentially corrupting of art. Waugh's prickly attitude to the modernist movement in popular culture is reflected in his general loathing of modernist art and comments on modernist contemporaries such as Joyce. In his work Waugh pilloried major modernist figures and movements from Le Corbusier to the surrealists for their pretensions and pomposity.[48] In style and method Waugh was like Orwell, an empiricist, committed to the clear and precise use of language.[49]

In a similar vein Orwell was hostile to unnecessary theoretical pretensions, and one of his most famous essays, 'The Politics of the English Language', is an attempt to defend the virtues of clarity and simplicity in style. For Orwell language became intrinsically connected with morality as he sought to defend principles of truth, objectivity and the verification of historical narratives, all things that he saw being systematically decimated during the 1930s on all sides. Both Orwell and Waugh associated theoretical pretension with obscurantism and intellectual elitism.[50] Critics have noted that Orwell's empiricism remained theoretically unsophisticated, a factor he would perhaps have been perfectly happy with.[51]

The reaction of both Waugh and Orwell to theoretical innovation were reflective of the tradition of British empiricism that has its roots in Hobbes, Locke and Hume. For many of its modern critics British empiricism is seen as an inherently conservative and outdated philosophy. This is hardly fair, in that empiricism was a sceptical philosophy that could generate radical and unsettling conclusions.[52] The work of Hume and Hobbes, as is well known, can be seen to call into question everything from a belief in god to the authority of religious and political institutions – hardly the position of the traditional conservative. Indeed, it is the coruscating relativism at the centre of this tradition that Waugh found most difficult to live with, finding only in Catholicism the absolutism and foundations that he felt necessary to secure social life in the modern world.[53] This kind of empiricism is a sceptical tradition that doubts the power of reason to resolve fundamental problems of social life.

By contrast both Cook and Morris owe debts to the surrealist tradition in their works. Cook's caricature of English eccentricity frequently evokes the rich tradition from Lear and Carroll to the Goons. Cook was a masterful deflator of pomposity and pretension in his work, and a number of pieces show his ability to ridicule theoretical pretension. His well-known 'pete'n'dud' sketch with Dudley Moore set in an unnamed Art Gallery illustrates this nicely.[54] In the sketch the two work their way through various classical works of art in a gentle, mocking and deeply affectionate parody of the impact of the opening up of classical art to the working classes. In the age of mass culture anyone and everyone can have an opinion on matters of high and low art, irrespective of education, upbringing and the quality of their judgments. Cook's ambivalent attitude to art and theory is almost a precursor to postmodern rejections of the division between high and low art; and it is with Morris that the tory anarchist fully enters the postmodern age. In works such as *Jam* and *Brass Eye* Morris is able to mix surrealist ideas with the mundane aspects of everyday life to force the viewer to revise radically the way in which they approach and interpret TV shows. Morris appears to share something of Baudrillard's view of the media as creating a 'hyper real' world where the difference between appearance and reality is abandoned, as popular culture becomes a realm of continuous invention of the idea of what is real. As Patrick West noted, it is impossible to watch a TV current affairs show in the same way after viewing Morris's work.[55]

In practice – iconoclasm and profanity

The impact of tory anarchists on the public sphere in the UK has been immense and challenging. As noted earlier, one of the distinguishing aspects of tory anarchism is its unrelenting iconoclasm and rebellious nature. This manifests itself in a variety of ways, from affectionate caricatures of all social classes through to hostile and extreme attacks on religion and politics. There is something of the permanent adolescent about tory anarchists, the need to continually annoy and aggravate in order to gain attention.

Waugh was very much a rebel in his youth and early years as a writer. His relationship to 'anarchy' was complicated, though, in that he had both the impulse of the natural rebel whilst at the same time he was driven by a fear of nihilism and chaos, which in part inspired his conversion to Catholicism. In his novels Waugh creates an amoral and chaotic world where justice and morality have little place.[56]

In these works black comedy and satire become Waugh's defence against the nihilism that he feared was an inevitable outcome of modernity where atheism replaced faith.[57] The early satires were controversial for a number of reasons: their clear analysis and tacit defence of English racism, the venal nature of a corrupt and idiotic ruling class, the opportunistic nature of public figures, businessmen and politicians, the stupidity of religious figures, perverse sexual practices including paedophilia, all were ripe targets for Waugh's lacerating wit. But they were also things not much commented upon by members of his class at the time, let alone in such an open manner. Orwell noted of Waugh that he was 'about as good a novelist as one can be while holding untenable opinions.'[58] As an ironist Waugh's relationship to the things he satirised was ambiguous, as Orwell also noted. In exposing the corruption of culture Waugh was also defending things that were abhorrent to the socialist Orwell. For Waugh there is a sense in which these things simply *are* and as such they can only be mocked, satirised or celebrated as part of the true picture of England.

Orwell's impact is perhaps the greatest of any of the figures here, in ways that he could not have anticipated. In some respects this is a little surprising, in that his work is generally the least satirical of any of the tory anarchists mentioned here. Orwell's tory anarchist instincts were rendered more explicit in his short essays celebrating England and its cultural traditions. Nonetheless *Animal Farm* is now celebrated as one of the greatest of political satires. Together with the bleak *1984*, the book has had the greatest impact upon popular and political culture of any of Orwell's writings,[59] and is precisely in keeping with tory anarchism. Orwell believed in a public sphere that would enable people through the critical and precise use of language to see the true horror of totalitarianism and injustice, though, as he noted, being able to recognise what is in front of your nose is often the hardest of tasks.[60] The book was thus a polemic and a provocation, rubbing the audience's nose in the truth of what was. The hostility to the state, the defence of the individual and of liberty, the need to rebel against authority and conformism were his central themes. Initially – and ironically – Orwell had great trouble publishing *Animal Farm*, as the standard left-wing publishing houses of the time were not sympathetic to works that would be seen as attacks on Britain's erstwhile ally, Stalin.[61]

A superficial reading would suggest that Peter Cook's work is perhaps the least politicised of the tory anarchists featured here, but in fact Cook has had a lasting and important impact on British popular *and* political culture. His purchase of *Private Eye* magazine in 1964 was to prove far-sighted as it remains Britain's longest running and most notorious satirical magazine, and has, over the years, taken on every manner of bully, crook and cheat in public life, risking bankruptcy and imprisonment along the way. The weapons of *Private Eye* are straightforward: iconoclastic humour and relentless investigative reporting, personified in the work of former contributor Paul Foot. Ian Hislop, the current editor, insists that *Private Eye* has always been politically ecumenical but there is no doubt that it became a haven for tory anarchists, including former editor Richard Ingrams and Evelyn Waugh's son Auberon.[62] The tone of the magazine is very much infused with Cook's surreal humour and as long-term owner he was a regular contributor. Equally important however was Cook's earlier work with *Beyond the Fringe* and the 'Establishment Club', where satire as public performance became mainstream.[63] It is difficult to appreciate the bravery of Cook's stance now in mocking the Macmillan Government and the social mores of a conformist era, but his colleagues from *Beyond the Fringe* attested to this in a posthumous collection of essays and interviews on Cook's life and work.[64] Cook's influence over subsequent British comedy has been immense, and the notorious *Derek and Clive* records and film went on to break new ground in scatological humour, opening the way for future comedians to broach the most extreme and taboo areas of life and language.

Throughout his career Cook remained a public figure, readily available to appear on chat shows and radio. Apparently wracked by almost terminal boredom and depression in his later life, his work varied from contributions to the Amnesty International Secret Policemen's Ball to what was at the time a series of relatively anonymous contributions to a late-night Radio London talk show where he would adopt the guise of 'Sven', a Norwegian migrant to Britain. Towards the end of his life he returned to a stock character, the aristocratic eccentric Sir Arthur Greeb-Streebling, for a series of often uncomfortable exchanges with Chris Morris on BBC Radio 4 in the show *Why Bother*? Morris adopts his customary persona to interrogate Sir Arthur and is unrelenting in his treatment of Cook, who by then was suffering badly from alcohol-related health problems.[65]

Cook's politics remain ambiguous and his friends straddled the political divide.[66] He was claimed equally by the right and the left, but it seems that he did at one point consider standing as a liberal candidate in Hampstead so that he could contest the seat with Labour's Glenda Jackson. Whether this was out of a deep-seated commitment to liberal principles or merely because it was an opportunity to poke fun at and deflate the political ambitions of Glenda Jackson is less clear.[67]

Morris's work in the public sphere is wide-ranging and includes television and radio shows. I want to concentrate on his work *Brass Eye* and in particular the special edition produced in 2001 called 'Paedogeddon'. 'Paedogeddon' was a critique of the ways in which the media in Britain had covered and hyped fears about paedophiles in the community. More deeply it was an examination of the irresponsibility of the media, coupled with its manifest hypocrisy. The show provoked by pointing up the ways in which popular culture sexualises children, parading them in beauty pageants and in popular music, producing artists such as Britney Spears and Jennifer Lopez. These are not the Lolitas of Nabokov's work, but merely children being used by corporations as a means to sell goods to adults and children alike. The real threat to children comes from a culture where children gain value and respect from peers and adults by the extent of their sexual maturity. Needless to say, few of these points were raised in the media coverage of the show other than in a few articles in UK papers such as *The Independent*. Instead the programme was lambasted in predictable manner by press and politicians alike. Home Secretary David Blunkett condemned the show, and MP Beverley Hughes attacked the programme in the House of Commons – while at the same time acknowledging she hadn't actually watched it. The then culture secretary Tessa Jowell moved to have Channel 4 amend its constitution so that such a show could not be broadcast again. Amongst the hysterical and ridiculous press coverage pride of place goes to the tabloid *Daily Star* who condemned the programme under the heading 'Sick show goes on regardless', while on the adjacent page of the newspaper a picture of a buxom Charlotte Church is headed with the phrase 'She's a big girl now' and that the singer was looking 'chest swell'. Charlotte Church was 15 years old at the time.[68]

The *Brass Eye* special was a classic example of tory anarchist provocation, holding up a mirror to the hypocrisy of contemporary society without a need for a didactic moralism in order to make its point. Tellingly the show received the highest ever response from viewers at the time of broadcast, producing a record number of phone calls condemning the show, and a record number praising it. At least it can be said that the British public held to a more complex understanding of the programme than the media and political elites that almost uniformly condemned it.

In the subsequent and what appears to be one-off series *Nathan Barley*, Morris presents the eponymous star of the programme as symptomatic of a modern moral malaise. Nathan Barley is a 'webmaster, guerrilla filmmaker, screenwriter, DJ and in his own words, a "self-facilitating media node".' In fact as a new media figure Barley is concerned only with feeding his own ego and desires and has no qualms about how he achieves fame or gratification, whether it is through sex with a thirteen-year-old girl, the trivialising of rape or the unintended killing of his colleague: all are fair game for Barley in his quest to become a cool celebrity. Barley himself is a former public school boy, one of Waugh's 'bright young things' brought up to date, the logical outcome of eighty years of decadence and debauchery amongst the upper classes in modern Britain. Although Morris doesn't appear in the programme, it is hard not to think that he is represented by the forlorn hero of the show, Dan Ashcroft. As the programme's website says of Ashcroft,:'[he] writes searing columns for Sugar Ape. He's considered astonishingly cool, but only by those he despises. He is surrounded by idiots and practically worshipped by Nathan (whom he considers to be their king). He is 34. Why has he failed to move on?'[69] Oh the irony indeed.

KICKING AGAINST THE PRICKS? THE LIMITATIONS OF TORY ANARCHISM

The biggest problem in writing about tory anarchists is that at any moment an analysis can be undermined by the claim that they are, as Roger Law put it, just 'arsing around.' In a sense this is of course true, tory anarchists are permanent adolescents who do indeed enjoy arsing around. My point in this paper is two-fold, that they are doing more than this and that their cultural criticism is something that requires explanation. My explanation is that tory anarchism emerges in the context of and in reaction to the relative decline of the UK (more specifically England) as a global power and with it the changing meaning of British identity. As a consequence there is no reason to suppose that tory anarchism will disappear from British culture, as the particularities of the UK's decline and social transformation continue to generate the grounds for its existence. The permanent tension that exists in tory anarchism is between the recognition that the world is always potentially chaotic and the need for certainty for society to function; between its rebellious impulse and its defence of the natural order of things. At its extreme this means the tension between the alternatives of nihilism or authority, with satire as the means to negotiate this spectrum. As this article has made clear, tory anarchists have particular strengths, but these are also, in turn, part of their inherent weakness as cultural critique.

Taking its strengths first: tory anarchism is first and foremost an important source of rebellion in British culture. It shows that rebellion does not have to be the product of the oppressed but that it can emerge from amongst the privileged too, rebelling against the failings of their own class and culture. Tory anarchists provide an alternative commentary on capitalism, modernity and the state, setting out their shortcomings from a position that is rooted in defence of a conception of Britain that is both appealing and illusory. Perhaps its most important strength is that it brings humour into the realm of cultural critique as a weapon to deflate the pretensions of the pompous, the over-mighty and the arrogant. In a world driven by the ambitions of a puritan political class and a utilitarian economic class, tory anarchism is a refreshing defence of indulgence, disorder, idleness, quality of life over quantity – what Cobbett called 'Merrie England' – and endless eccentricity.

At the same time the limitations of tory anarchism are apparent. Orwell aside, their anti-political stance is unlike left-wing anarchism in that there is no sense of a political alternative to what exists, no desire to promote a different conception of a good society. Being a tory anarchist has built-in limitations, it is a minority sport rather than a social or political movement. Its social ideas rest on an appealing and partial vision of 'Merrie England' that exists only as a myth in British culture, albeit an important one. While the tory anarchist rails against capitalism for its debasement of social values, against the state for its erosion of liberty and sweeping social engineering, and against modernity for its attempts to build a good society on the basis of abstract reason, it doesn't offer a coherent analysis of these issues. The purpose of tory anarchism is to be bloody-minded in defence of the indefensible and to expose society's hypocrisies and vices to public gaze, to laugh at, rather than condemn them, and invite others to start laughing too. Although it doesn't comment directly on abstractions such as the UK's decline in the world system, tory anarchism tells us much about this process indirectly, and in a way that mixes the tragic and the hilarious in an ongoing commentary on the changing nature of British culture. For that it deserves its place in the annals of British political and popular culture.

Thanks to Samantha Wood for her help in researching this article. Also thanks to John Roberts, Mark Lacy, Lloyd Pettiford and the reviewers for their helpful comments.

NOTES

1. Waugh says that 'satire is a matter of period. It flourishes in a stable society and presupposes homogeneous moral standards ... It is aimed at inconstancy and hypocrisy. It exposes polite cruelty and folly by exaggerating them. It seeks to produce shame'. Quoted in David Wykes, *Evelyn Waugh: A Literary life* (London, Macmillan, 1999), 7. Waugh rejected the idea that he was a satirist.
2. John Gray and David Willets, *Is Conservatism Dead*, 40.
3. R. J. White, *The Conservative Tradition* (London: Nicholas Kaye, 1950), 36.
4. Patrick West argues that tory anarchists can be found in many parts of English society. I am agnostic on this point but my primary concern is with the tory anarchist as public figure. Email to the author dated 22 November 2005.
5. On Swift's mixture of libertarian and conservative views see Ian Higgins, *Swift's Politics* (Cambridge, Cambridge University Press, 1994), 67. See also Milton's *Areopagitica*, for example. On William Cobbett see Richard Ingrams, *The Life and Adventures of William Cobbett* (London, Harper Perennial, 2005).
6. On the death of conservatism see John Gray, *The Undoing of Conservatism* (London, The Social Market Foundation, 1994). See his exchanges with David Willets for a challenge to this idea, in *Is Conservatism Dead?* (London: The Social Market Foundation, 1997).
7. Immanuel Wallerstein, *After Liberalism* (New York, The New Press, 1995).
8. Ian Gilmour was a leading UK Conservative Party 'wet', sacked by Mrs. Thatcher and an outspoken critic of her administrations. He set out a coherent overview of the history of conservatism in the UK in *Inside Right: Conservatism, Policies and the People* (London, Quarter Books, 1978); and *Whatever Happened to the Tories?* (with Mark Garnett) (London, Fourth Estate Paperbacks, 1997).
9. Waugh and Orwell held each other's work in mutual regard. See Timothy Garton Ash

'Orwell in 1998', *The New York Review of Books*, 22 October 1998; John P. Rossie, 'Two irascible Englishmen: Mr. Waugh and Mr. Orwell', *Modern Age*, 22 March 2005, 148-152.

10. Selina Hastings, *Evelyn Waugh* (London, Vintage, 2002).
11. Malcolm Bradbury, *Evelyn Waugh* (Edinburgh and London: Oliver and Boyd, 1966), 16-17.
12. On Orwell see Bernard Crick, *George Orwell: A Life*; Michael Sheldon, *Orwell: The Authorised Biography* (London, HarperCollins, 1991); Jeffrey Meyers, *Orwell: Conscience of a Generation* (London, W. W. Norton, 2000).
13. Orwell, ever sensitive to the layers of social class, saw himself as being born into a 'lower-upper-middle class family'. Timothy Garton Ash, 'Orwell in 1998.' See D. J. Taylor for a detailed account of Orwell on class, *Orwell: The Life* (London, Random House, 2003).
14. Like Waugh, Cook denied that he was a satirist. John Bird makes the case for this interpretation of much of Cook's work in '3. The Last Pieces' in *Something Like Fire: Peter Cook Remembered*, 210.
15. Morris has commented in interview that he grew up near Huntingdon, attended 'public school to get the right accent, catholic school to get the right guilt complex.'
16. Morris has been scornful of the ways in which satire has become institutionalised in Britain through shows such as 'Have I got news for you', because of their collusion with the establishment they claim to criticise. Morris said, by contrast, 'I think you can only really get underneath by deception.' Euan Ferguson, *The Observer*, 22 July 2001.
17. *George Orwell at Home (and among the Anarchists)* (London, Freedom Press, 1998), 17. Orwell was clearly sympathetic to anarchism in theory but in practice thought it impossible to bring about, as Vernon Richards, Colin Ward and Nicolas Walter note in their essays in the book. Orwell regularly referred to himself as a tory anarchist, as is noted by many of his biographers including Bernard Crick, *George Orwell: A Life* (London, Penguin, 1982), 174; Gordon Bowker, *George Orwell*, (London, Little Brown, 2003), 154 and 174.
18. Evelyn Waugh, *The Ordeal of Gilbert Pinfold* (London, Penguin, 1972 edition), 14.
19. George Orwell, 'Fascism and Democracy', in his *Collected Essays, Journalism and Letters: My country, right or left: 1940-43*, (London, David R. Godine Publishers, 2000).
20. Patrick West makes this point when he says the 'tory anarchist laughs at the human

condition because we despair often of its cruelty and ignorance ... In my opinion Morris so brutally satirised anti-paedophile campaigns because, like myself, he felt disgusted at the cretinous and blood-thirsty behaviour of "anti-paedo" lynch-mobs.' Email to the author dated 22 November 2005.

21. On Cook's life and times see Harry Thompson, *Peter Cook: A Biography.*
22. Declan McHugh, 'Wanting to be heard but not wanting to act? Addressing political disengagement', in *Parliamentary Affairs*, 59, 3, 2006: 546.
23. Timothy Garton Ash, 'Orwell in 1998'.
24. On Waugh and Orwell's relationship to the end of empire and issues of class see Christopher Hitchens, *Blood, Class and Nostalgia* (London, Chatto and Windus, 1990).
25. Accessible atwww.online-literature.com/orwell/887/ and www.orwell.ru/library/articles/hanging/english/e_hanging
26. Selina Hastings, *Evelyn Waugh*, 227.
27. On the Establishment club see John Bird in *Something Like Fire: Peter Cook Remembered* (London, Arrow Books, 2003). See also Peter Barberis, 'The 1964 General Election the "Not Quite, But" and "But only Just" Election', *Contemporary British History*, 21, 3, 2007, for an account of the satire boom inaugurated by Cook and his cohorts on the party political culture of the time.
28. Nicholas Luard in *Something Like Fire: Peter Cook Remembered*, 39.
29. See the chapters by Alan Bennett and Nicholas Luard in *Something Like Fire: Peter Cook Remembered.*
30. Waugh commented that 'the most valuable possession of any nation is an accepted system of classes', *The Sayings of Evelyn Waugh*, 41.
31. Edmund Burke shared this view of class. See Noel O'Sullivan, *Conservatism*, (London: J. M. Dent and Son, 1976), 12.
32. David Wykes, *Evelyn Waugh*, 36.
33. Valerie J. Simms, 'A reconsideration of Orwell's 1984: The moral implication of despair', *Ethics*, vol. 84, no. 4, 1974, 303-306. Simms makes the important point of clarifying that Orwell viewed *1984* as a satirical warning of the possibility, not the inevitability, of the spread of totalitarianism.
34. According to long-time friend Roger Law, Cook's theory of satire was that everyone was a potential target, no subject could be taboo and that you should be completely unjust to those you were attacking. Cook, like Chris Morris, felt that to remain

credible as a professional you could never become cosy with the establishment for fear of losing your autonomy; see Harry Thompson, *Peter Cook: A Biography*, 297.

35. Former Tory Cabinet minister George Walden notes Mrs Thatcher's lack of enthusiasm for 'non-utilitarian studies', subjects that did not contribute directly to the economy, in George Walden, *Lucky George* (London, Allen Lane, 1999), 273.
36. Cook commented in interview that he found the Thatcher governments more offensive than any other, though it should be noted that he was liable to say different things to different friends on political issues; see Harry Thompson, *Peter Cook: A Life*, 295-296. On the relationship to the conservative tradition see R. J. White, *The Conservative Tradition*, 19-20 and Maurice Cowling's comments in Frank O'Gorman, *British Conservatism*, 227-228.
37. R. J. White, *The Conservative Tradition*, 47; Anthony Quinton, *The Politics of Imperfection* (London: Faber and Faber, 1978), 16; Ian Gilmour, *Inside Right*, 142-144.
38. Roger Scruton, *The Meaning of Conservatism* (London: The Macmillan Press, 1984), 38.
39. Interview with John Freeman for the BBC, 18 June 1960, http://www.bbc.co.uk/bbcfour/audiointerviews/profilepages/waughe1.shtml, last viewed 11/5/2007.
40. On conservative fears of rational bureaucracy see Robert Nisbet, *Conservatism: Dream and Reality* (Milton Keynes: Open University Press, 1991), 34-35.
41. Historically patriotism has tended to be regarded as a conservative idea against the more cosmopolitan and internationally inclined liberal, socialist and anarchist traditions. See Frank O'Gorman, *British Conservatism* (New York: Longman Group, 1986), xiii. Unlike Orwell, however, O'Gorman links patriotism with imperialism.
42. See, for example, Orwell's pamphlet *The Lion and the Unicorn; Socialism and the English Genius* (London, Penguin, 1982).
43. See Orwell, *The Road to Wigan Pier* (London, Penguin, 1975 edition), chapters 11-13.
44. John Gray and David Willets, *Is Conservatism Dead?*, p.viii.
45. Euan Ferguson reports one friend of Morris who says that the latter is motivated by 'pomposity of any type and stupidity'. Ferguson, *The Observer*.
46. See George Walden's *The New Elites: Making a Career in the masses* (London, Penguin, 2000) for a persuasive conservative defence of high values against populism in art.

47. Brooke Allen, 'Vile Bodies: A Futurist Fantasy', *Twentieth Century Literature*, 40, 3, 1994, 318-328.
48. Nisbet notes that conservatives have always been alert to the dangers of populism in art and culture, Nisbet, *Conservatism*, 92.
49. David Wykes, *Evelyn Waugh,* 4. On Waugh's method see his letter to Robin Campbell in *The Letters of Evelyn Waugh*, edited by Mark Amory (London, Phoenix, 1995), 215.
50. Waugh was a strict defender of good grammar and clear expression. See his comments on Stephen Spender in Simon Whitechapel, 'Relative Values', *Evelyn Waugh Newsletter and Studies,* last viewed 1-11-2007.
51. Terry Eagleton, 'Reach-me-down Romantic', *The London Review of Books*, 19 June, 2003.
52. Stephen Priest, *The British Empiricists*, (London, Penguin, 1990).
53. On Waugh's Catholicism see the interview in 'The Art of Fiction No. 30', *Paris Match*, 1962.
54. William Cook (editor), *Tragically I was an only Twin* (London, Arrow Books, 2003), 116-121.
55. Email from West to the author dated 22 November 2005, where West says of Morris: 'Chris Morris's main contribution is that he has changed the way many of us look at the media. His television programmes *The Day Today* (co-written with Armando Ianucci) and *Brass Eye* mercilessly exposed the way the media create stories, manipulate the viewers through devious editing and absurd graphics, and employ meaningless jargon. Most people will never read Marshall McLuhan or Jean Baudrillard, but Morris has done more to make a generation appreciate that what they see reported on television is not transparent and objective. As one of the graphics on *The Day Today* said in a spirit of self-refutation: "Fact times interpretation equals truth", as if to say "truth" was a scientific entity.'
56. Malcolm Bradbury, *Evelyn Waugh* (Edinburgh and London, Oliver and Boyd, 1966), 24.
57. Michael Gorra, 'Through comedy towards Catholicism: A reading of Evelyn Waugh's early novels', *Contemporary Literature*, 29, 2, 1988, 202.
58. Christopher Hitchens, 'The Permanent Adolescent', *The Atlantic Monthly*, May 2003.
59. Terry Eagleton, in 'Reach-me-down Romantic'; Geoffrey Wheatcroft in 'Look right, look left, look right again', *New Statesman*, 2 April, 1999; and biographer D. J. Taylor, *Orwell: The Life*, 410.

60. George Orwell, 'In front of your nose', in his *Collected Essays: Journalism and Letters – In front of your nose, 1945-50, Vol. 4* (London, Penguin, 1993).
61. An interesting historical irony here is that Jonathon Cape rejected the manuscript after having initially accepted it, on the advice of an official from the Ministry of Information who subsequently turned out to be a Soviet spy, D. J Taylor, *Orwell: The Life*, 337.
62. Email from Ian Hislop to the author, 22 November 2005.
63. Christopher Booker provides an orthodox conservative commentary on this period in *The Neophiliacs* (London, William Collins and Sons. Ltd, 1970), 99, where he notes that 'the upper classes in England had in fact been losing faith in their traditional values, and bourgeois self-confidence, for over half a century'.
64. See Harry Thompson, *Peter Cook: A Biography*, for a detailed account of Cook's early career with Beyond the Fringe, the Establishment and the Cambridge Footlights. Also, John Wells, 'The Mystic Spube' in *Something Like Fire: Peter Cook Remembered.*
65. See William Cook, *Tragically I was an only Twin*.
66. Nicholas Luard suggests that Cook was seduced by socialism in the 1960s but came to reject it and adopt a 'small "c"' conservatism for the rest of his life, *Peter Cook: Something Like Fire*, 42. See also Harry Thompson, *Peter Cook: A Biography*, 81, for an account of Cook's distrust of radical politics.
67. Adrian Slade, 'Peter Cook: Thirty Seven Years a very rare friend', in *Something Like Fire: Peter Cook Remembered*, 18.
68. *Daily Star*, page 6, 8 September 2001.
69. *Nathan Barley*, Channel Four, , last viewed 11/05/2007.

Anarchist Studies 17.1 © 2009 ISSN 0976 3393
www.lwbooks.co.uk/journals/anarchiststudies/

'Love is always free': anarchism, free unions, and utopianism in Edwardian England

Ginger Frost

Department of History
Samford University
Birmingham, Alabama 35229
USA

gsfrost@samford.edu

ABSTRACT

This article analyzes the Anarchist attitude to marriage and free unions in England in the fin-de-siecle by examining two relationships – that of Guy Aldred and Rose Witcop and Rudolf Rocker and Milly Witcop. Anarchist rhetoric about marriage was trenchant and uncompromising; marriage was legalized prostitution and unworthy of truly free individuals. In practice, however, anarchists were more flexible, accepting that hostile circumstances required adjustments. In fact, both of these couples legally married, though for different reasons. Because most anarchists believed in (at least) serial monogamy and in heterosexuality, they had fewer alternatives to marriage from which to choose. In addition, in the end, what mattered most was the relationship between the couple, not its legal form. Ironically, the group most associated with 'free love' actually practiced it rarely, not from timidity but from a respect for individual rights, particularly for women members.

Keywords: *marriage, free union, utopianism, woman question, individualism*

Nineteenth-century critics often dismissed anarchism as utopian in the negative sense of being overly optimistic about human nature, about the likely impact of their theoretical ideas on the lives of real people, and about the possibility of being able to find alternative, non-hierarchical ways of living. The critique was frequently supplemented by the charge that anarchism threatened social dissolution. Anarchists championed individual freedom more than other socialists; some anarchists argued that no social concerns should interfere with the rights of the individual.[1] Naturally, the anarchist movement that emerged in 1880s Britain was diverse. Renewed by constant waves of émigrés from all over Europe – including Prince Peter Kropotkin and Louise Michel – anarchists benefited from the rise of syndicalism in the years before World War I and worked in conjunction with other radical organizations, for example William Morris's Socialist League. A few Tolstoyan communities also formed, living off of the land and their own labour; the colony of Whiteway, in the Cotswolds, was the best known example.[2]

Nevertheless, what distinguished the anarchists from other revolutionaries was a commitment to individualism as well as socialism and a belief that coercion could play no part in a just society. In politics, this commitment translated to a rejection of the power of the state as well as the oppression of capitalism. This did not necessarily imply the elimination of all governance, but required authoritative decisions to rise from below rather than be imposed from above, usually through the organization of federated communes. What did it imply in social relations? Though anarchist writings concerned themselves primarily with issues of capitalism and state power, anarchists also had well-worked ideas about marriage and gender relations. Some attempted to put these ideas into practice and live by their principles. Their experiences – if inspired by utopian dreams – suggested a degree of practicality and realism ignored by the critics. Indeed, more consistently than other groups, anarchists faced up squarely to the issues of freedom and responsibility in private life, and, rather than simply theorize how life ought to be, they attempted to work out how they might build ideal relationships in less than ideal settings.

Studying anarchist experiences of free unions is difficult, first, because so much information about them comes from hostile sources, and second, because the sources are fragmentary. In order to get around this difficulty, this article will focus on two couples who experimented with free unions in the Edwardian period and who also left writings explaining their decisions – Guy Aldred and

Rose Witcop and Rudolf Rocker and Milly Witcop. Since Rose and Milly left few writings of their own, the analysis of these marital experiences will center primarily on the accounts left by the men, Rocker and Aldred. Each man had a distinct set of expectations about gender and cohabitation that showed the openness and variety of anarchist approaches to these issues, as well as the difficulties of creating successful unions. Both men believed in communism and anarchism and both argued for equality between men and women. Neither supported marriage but both believed in monogamy. Thus, their free unions were actually fairly conservative. Despite having these things in common, their approaches to living in free unions were different, as were the results of their experiments. In the end, both unions floundered, owing to weakness in the relationships (in the case of Guy and Rose) and, in both cases, because of institutional pressures. Yet whilst neither union was an unmitigated success, it is possible to see the *attempt* to realize free love as a successful experiment in utopianism, showing that anarchists were not bound by a rigid adherence to theory and that even dogmatic anarchists like Aldred could be flexible in dealing with difficult real-life issues.

THE WOMAN QUESTION: SOCIALISM, FEMINISM AND ANARCHISM

A widespread interest in issues of marriage and the family emerged in the late Victorian and Edwardian era. These were decades of profound dissatisfaction with the Victorian family and gender roles. Feminists and socialists struggled with how best to accommodate the needs of men, women, and children within marriage. Neither group entirely succeeded in defining the ideal relationship. For example, whilst acknowledging the subordination of women within marriage, women's rights workers remained unenthusiastic about eliminating it. As Lucy Bland has pointed out, most feminists 'did not reject marriage *per se*. On the contrary, they wished it to be radically reformed.' Women's rights advocates argued against the sexual double standard not to free women's sexuality but to demand chastity from men. And despite the increasingly trenchant rhetoric, few were prepared to enter into free unions, since they saw cohabitation as an opportunity for male sexual aggression; marriage was women's only protection from unscrupulous men. Many women concentrated on removing married women's legal disabilities and on convincing men that they must change as well as women in order for marriage to work.[3]

Socialists were also critical of marriage, but similarly ambivalent about replacing it. They primarily objected to two things, both already identified by the Owenites in the early nineteenth century: the disabilities marriage imposed on women and the indissolubility of marriage. What to do about marriage laws, though, was a vexed issue. Socialists argued that marriage arrangements mirrored the economic system; in other words, the capitalist system required monogamy in order to secure male property rights. Under communism, such property in women would no longer be necessary. Couples, then, could enter and exit unions as they saw fit, with no interference from the state.[4] Thus, in theory, the elimination of capitalism promised to solve the 'woman problem.' Yet working this out in terms of policy in Victorian and Edwardian England was a different matter. Arguments in the Social Democratic Federation (SDF) illustrated the problem. As Karen Hunt's work has shown, the SDF could only deal with the issue of women's rights and free unions by leaving the question open to individual conscience and letting individual members take their own positions. Indeed, the leadership did not want the party to be associated with notorious free unions, fearing a loss of support from the working-class masses. Other socialist organizations were similarly compromised; the Independent Labour Party, for instance, was actively hostile to any marital nonconformity, since they wanted to attract as large a following as possible.[5]

Anarchist critiques of marriage had both similarities and differences with those advanced by social democrats and feminists. Leading figures in the movement recognized the need to combine social justice with individual freedom. In this way, they were more realistic than their critics acknowledged, utopian only insofar as they envisioned a better world for the majority of people. Moreover, they did not invariably prioritize theoretical solutions over the everyday challenges of ordinary people. This was particularly true on the issue of marriage. Unlike most feminists and socialists, anarchists did not simply theorize; many of them lived out their ideals, openly confronting the difficulties of free unions in a hostile legal and social environment. Though anarchist writings set high goals and ideals, their actions were practical, and they were realistic about the need for both freedom and responsibility in relations between men and women.

Anarchist critiques of marriage were trenchant and, in rhetoric, uncompromising. Anarchists wanted to limit restrictions over everyday life and argued that control of people's intimate lives was illegitimate and unnecessary. Many of them asserted that marriage was just one more conventional vehicle of oppression that should be abandoned. As R.M. Fox put it, anarchists did not 'believe in the Institution of Marriage anymore than they believed in the Institution of the King.' Indeed, some anarchists asserted the right of cohabitants to change partners at will, since 'variety' was necessary 'both for man and for woman.' This was not, however, a majority view.[6] More commonly, anarchists insisted that love could not be coerced; any contract that bound people together without regard to feeling was by definition immoral. A writer in *The Anarchist* expressed this view in the following terms: 'There is no such love that is not free, and all forced love, or unreal love, such as the laws and institution of marriage only exist to maintain, is prostitution alone, and nothing better.' On this view, free unions had a better chance of success than marriage, and it chimed in with the general importance anarchists attached to individual liberty, distinguishing them from other socialists and many feminists. Nellie Shaw, who cohabited with Francis Sedlak at Whiteway, argued that unions that depended 'entirely on the honour and love of the parties concerned ... were far more likely to be enduring.'[7]

Notwithstanding the differences between anarchists and feminists, anarchists argued for free unions *because* of their support for women's rights. The marriage contract enshrined women's subordination, making her a chattel; no self-respecting woman would sign such an agreement. In this, anarchists echoed the sentiments expressed by the Owenites fifty years before. Unless they cohabited in free unions, the choice facing women was between married or unmarried prostitution. The anarchist press was full of cries that '[t]he courtesan is sexually free; the wife is a slave,' and '[t]he emancipation of woman from her domestic slavery is to be found in the abolition of the marriage laws.' In addition, as Nellie Shaw pointed out, anarchist women disliked marriage because it 'gave the right over the children to the father, who alone was regarded as "parent,"' so they 'preferred to have the control of the children ...' In other words, they recognized that, in some ways, a mistress had the legal advantage over a wife. Henry Seymour, a leading individualist anarchist, did not even think the law should enforce parental responsibilities, since women could use birth control and buy insurance policies, if necessary. But he did not think this would be necessary in anarchy because '[l]iberty creates free men and women, and crime and cowardice are incompatible with liberty.'[8]

Because the movement was so fractured and because of the resistance to the formulation of policy, the practical approaches anarchists adopted on the marriage question and free unions varied enormously between and within groups. Some couples tried free unions only in communal settings, where worries about child care and the possible desertion of women were lessened, as at Whiteway. Others stressed the importance of legal marriage while English society remained unreformed; many of the movement's leading writers, such as Henry Seymour and Peter Kropotkin, were legally wed. Still others pioneered free unions as individual family units, despite the hostile environment. In this, all but a small minority rejected promiscuity. 'Free love,' they asserted, was a misnomer; most wanted the church and state out of their private lives, but few envisaged anything more radical than unregulated monogamy. Yet the term 'free love' was open to interpretation, and the meaning different anarchists attached to the concept often only became clear through lived experience.

ALDRED, ROCKER AND THE WITCOPS

One of the best-documented anarchist relationships was that of Guy Aldred and Rose Witcop. The two lived in a free union between 1908 and 1921, an apparently mutual decision, since both held strong critiques of marriage and women's position in Edwardian England. Aldred was born in London in 1886, the barely legitimate son of a naval officer and a parasol maker. Guy went through a quick succession of careers as preacher, office boy and free-lance journalist. In 1907, after he had converted to atheism and anarchism, he met Rose at a social event. Witcop's birth name was Rachel Witkopski, and she came to Britain with her family in the large wave of Eastern European Jewish immigrants at the turn of the century, fleeing the persecution of the Tsar in Polish Russia. Witcop was only seventeen when she met Aldred, but she was already a poised and accomplished worker in radical movements. An ardent feminist and supporter of workers' rights, she had worked in the East End of London amongst some of the poorest and most sweated workers. The couple quickly fell in love, and though their courtship was chaste for some time – in conformity with mainstream social mores – they both had unconventional ideas about love and marriage.[9]

Aldred's disdain for legal marriage was one of his firmest articles of faith. His own parents had never lived together, and both of them married bigamously later in their lives, a circumstance that made Guy deeply skeptical about the sanctity of marriage and his parents' 'respectability.' He wrote in 1908, '[c]apitalism should be opposed since it does not work. The same thing applies to marriage ... The English law of marriage I consider both objectionable and stupid. Personally, I do not believe in marriage laws at all ...' Aldred's parents' hypocrisy especially disgusted him. He condemned his mother's bigamy by saying that 'she wanted to do wrong and she wanted to do it decently.' His father was even worse, since his bigamous marriage was in a church so was 'a magnificent blasphemous falsehood.' (His mother's bigamous marriage was at the Holborn Register Office.) He further excoriated his father's conventional friends who buried him under a false name (Arthur Rosebery) because 'they believed in the marriage laws.' He concluded, '[a]fter having concealed the actual crimes and wrongs of the marriage system, after having hidden a host of illegitimate relationships from public view, the defenders of the marriage system cry in chorus: "Behold! It works!" I have no patience with such scandalous hypocrisy.'[10]

Aldred's objection to marriage concerned more than its dishonesty; like many anarchists, he found a promise to love someone forever absurd. He insisted that '[t]here was nothing immoral in two people meeting and not promising to mate for life. The promise was void from the very start for neither party knew if it would hold for life.' Aldred, also a communist, further believed that a total overhaul of the economic system was necessary for women to have complete liberation.[11] Indeed, his feminism was another reason for his disdain for marriage. Like many reformers, he equated marriage with 'legalised prostitution' and 'rape by contract.' He pointed out married women's legal disabilities, which he termed 'serfdom,' and argued for 'a pure and simple form of free love.' In his opinion, freethinkers and socialists had a duty to attack marriage because of its harmful aspects towards women; in fact, he argued that '[s]ocialism must of necessity, if carried to its logical conclusion, involve an adherence to the principles of free love.'[12]

Aldred had some eccentric beliefs about marriage. For instance, he railed against the requirement that women change their names to that of their husbands, a position he took almost to the point of monomania. He protested that this change denied their individuality and proved that in a legal marriage, a woman's 'function was to be a chattel.' In addition, because of his background, he could argue that the problems with legal marriages were much worse than those of free unions: 'The defenders of the "shot-gun" wedding, or of the equally immoral careful property-secured alliance, have no right to attack either the irresponsibility or the materialism of the upholders of Free Mating.'[13] In fact, Aldred's own mother had been deserted after a legal marriage, as well as her bigamous one; the institution had not protected her or her child. Aldred concluded, 'I do not believe in desertion, either of human beings or of causes. Nor do I believe in institutions that are wrecked once the truth is proclaimed.' All the same, he insisted that he was not arguing for promiscuity: 'I do not believe in Free Love as an excuse for license.' He believed that 'the desire for monogamy' was increasing, and this would not change even if there were no marriage laws. Going even further, Aldred insisted that celibacy was on the increase and would eventually predominate among the most 'evolved' part of humanity.[14]

Rose Witcop left little writing of her own, though she was clearly in agreement with Aldred on many of these points. As Guy put it, she believed 'love must be free and could not be bound.' She was a socialist-anarchist first and a feminist second when that she met Aldred. She wrote a piece for the *Voice of Labour* arguing that economic changes to help the working class were far more important than women's suffrage at the present time. However, in this article she argued that each woman must realize that 'she is a slave in every sense of the word both in the factory and in her household.' In a letter to the *Freewoman* she also defended the practice of 'free love,' by asserting that 'there is a distinction between the terms lust, license, prostitution, and free love ... freewomen are not led by men, nor wish to lead men.' Instead of license, Witcop insisted people should enjoy relationships of 'staunch friendship, unsullied by obligations and duties, ties and certificates.' Thus whilst rejecting license, Witcop wanted sexual freedom: she had an adventurous and unapologetic sex life herself and later worked with Margaret Sanger for birth control reform. She was also the more assertive of the two, at least according to Aldred. Notwithstanding his preference for chastity, Rose gave birth to their son in 1909, so clearly she had her way on this as on many other matters.[15]

Aldred and Witcop's difficult relationship illustrated the challenges to free unions, especially as they did not entirely agree on what this relationship meant. Aldred claimed in his memoirs that Witcop had an affair early in their relationship and continued to do so often afterwards. When he went to prison for seditious libel in 1910, Rose stood by him and brought him books and writing materials. All the same, she also lived with another anarchist, E. F. Mylius, during that time, and Mylius informed Aldred of the affair when the latter was released from prison. Though Guy insisted repeatedly that he was not jealous, the relationship did not survive her infidelities, though they did not formally break off their union until after World War I. The two also eventually disagreed on politics. Specifically, Rose regarded nationalism as a bourgeois idea, irrelevant to anarchism, but Guy was more sympathetic, especially in the case of India. In addition, as Rose spent more of her time on birth control reform, Aldred became more critical. Though he supported the movement, he argued that socialism alone could solve the problem of unwanted births. As he later put it, she 'objected to my extreme Communism, and I objected to her birth control activities.' One of their associates, John McGovern, wrote that they were clearly breaking up when Guy was in prison in 1921, since they had 'many stormy scenes which took place between them in front of the warders.'[16]

In addition to these personal factors, the couple demonstrated the larger problems any member of a free union faced in the early twentieth century. Both Witcop and Aldred saw a great deal of family opposition. Guy's mother was anti-Semitic and also feared losing her son's economic support. Despite her own bigamous marriage, Mrs. Aldred also disapproved of the union on moral grounds, which understandably exasperated Guy. As he put it, '[m]y mother believed in marriage and all the hypocrisy of male-dominated society.' She never relented in her furious dislike of Witcop, even though Aldred continued to support his mother financially until he went to prison. Guy also lost touch with his three half-brothers, though this was largely due to circumstance rather than political differences (one died in World War I and the other two went to Canada). Rose's family was equally hostile; her mother was particularly distressed as Rose was the third of the four daughters in the family to reject legal wedlock. Mrs. Witcop further disliked that Aldred was not Jewish (a neat reversal of Guy's mother's reaction) and that he was an atheist. Nor did Polly and Milly, her two sisters, ever much like Guy, and, according to Aldred, none of Rose's family visited her after she gave birth to their son.[17] Only Guy's grandfather was supportive, since 'He approved of mating for love and not for money. And he did not think ceremony or state registration mattered if we each had the courage to stand firm.' Milly and Polly eventually came round, though they remained unenthusiastic about Guy himself.[18]

The couple also experienced many social difficulties. One night when they were out walking together, a policeman accused Rose of being a prostitute. Aldred protested vehemently and threatened to lodge a complaint so the constable apologized, but Rose was 'much upset.' Guy was also stigmatized, since he gained the reputation of being a 'free lover' – and with a girl in her teens. His mother refused to walk out with him, and acquaintances began to avoid him, believing him a cad. Landladies registered protests, though sometimes this had more to do with Guy and Rose's anarchism than their marital status. In addition, when Rose went into the hospital to give birth, the hospital authorities would not let Guy see Rose or the baby 'and treated her as "a fallen woman" ... They allowed no information as to her progress or that of the child to be vouchsafed to me.' (Aldred noted sarcastically, however, that they had no problem identifying him as her 'husband' when they wanted to send the bill.) The issue of names continued to plague the couple whenever they had dealings with private or governmental institutions. When Guy was in prison, the authorities would not allow Witcop to visit him unless she did so in the guise of 'Rose Witcop-Aldred.' Rose refused to do so, which led to a stand off. Eventually, the authorities relented and allowed her to see Guy as 'Rose Witcop' on the written form, but, 'the warders shouted always: "Mrs. Aldred to see Guy Aldred,"' when she got to the cells.[19]

The union's ultimate collapse was not a surprise given this environment. Ironically, the problems and possibilities of their experiment garnered publicity most in 1926, when Rose was threatened with deportation and the couple married. Justifying the expedient, Aldred said: 'I do not believe in the law of husband and wife. I do not believe in a woman taking a man's name and nationality. But since she does so under existing laws, I considered my former comrade's protection from deportation a duty ...'[20] His dissent from the monopoly of marriage was outweighed by his concern for the needs of the individual, in this case the mother of his son. For her part, Rose had lived an unusually free life, personally and politically, in part because of her class, but also because of her feminism and devotion to birth control. Unlike some women she had controlled her fertility successfully and had not limited herself to one sexual partner. She did not marry when she became pregnant, so she was not concerned about the stigma of unwed motherhood. Being a working-class woman, and a member of several radical societies, she did not have much to fear socially. But legally, her position was always problematic, as was that of her son, who was 'parentless at law.' The threat of deportation forced her to marry, and she was fortunate that Guy remained devoted to their son even after their break up. Many women in similar circumstances had to bear the expenses of child-rearing alone.

Aldred had been conscious of the difficulties the couple faced from the start of the relationship. Before he moved in with Rose, he wondered, '[w]ould each partner to the union remain the person the other mated? Would taking each other for granted destroy the romance that had inspired the mating?'[21] Later in his life, Aldred argued that love was not enough to make a relationship work; the couple must suit each other as well. Wisdom was as important as affection. From today's perspective the conclusion is hardly startling. But it points to Guy's insight into the problem of stability in the absence of restrictive marriage laws.

The Aldred-Witcop union foundered in part because neither partner was consistent about what s/he wanted. Aldred argued for chastity and monogamy, believing these to be the more 'evolved' versions of human relationships, yet he also wanted total emotional and sexual freedom for both partners. His stress on monogamy, in particular, sat uneasily with his insistence that people could not promise to mate for life, since they had no idea if they would always love each other. If this was true, how could monogamy be 'natural'? After all, if people were monogamous, then the bonds of matrimony would not pose difficulties, since they would stay together anyway. Presumably, Guy believed that the future 'evolution' of humans would erase these seeming contradictions, but that was little help for those living in unions in the present, including Guy himself. Rose was also contradictory, saying she did not believe in promiscuity, yet having numerous sexual partners while ostensibly still with Guy. That her own freedom of action compromised her partners' freedom did not stop her from doing as she pleased. Rose acted out her ideas of individual freedom, but at the cost of ending her 'staunch friendship' with Aldred.

Aldred suffered greatly from the failure of the relationship, and his autobiography is extremely touchy on the issue. He repeats over and over again that the union with Rose was purer and braver than any others. A typical passage is the following:

> Our association was definitely one of principle and challenge. This fact, a most virtuous and important fact in my opinion, placed our union far above most of the eccentric matings that occurred in the Socialist and Anarchist movement. The other unions were usually alliances of convenience that hid the facts from the world. We had nothing to hide. We challenged. Consequently, we met with a certain degree of persecution. And all because we believed in the ethical value of a true association of principle.[22]

Was he protesting too much? In a similar vein he argued that theirs was the first union that was both open and was not forced upon them: 'There was *no* legal and no *moral* barrier to our going through a ceremony. We refrained simply because we wished to assert and to challenge. In this matter we towered over our contemporaries and our predecessors.'[23] This remark showed a breathtaking dismissal of other couples and perhaps a need to feel superior despite the failure of the relationship. (He was particularly critical of Eleanor Marx's union with Edward Aveling, seeing her as a 'slave' and a hypocrite for taking Aveling's name. Clearly, the sectarianism of radical politics bled over into his views of private life.) Yet whilst Aldred had suffered the real disadvantages accruing to a man in love with a partner who exercises genuine sexual freedom and was, as a result, possibly too proud to admit that this had bothered him, to his credit he also remained faithful to the principle of free unions. After Rose's death in 1932, he entered a second free union with Jenny Patrick, who worked with him in his various presses. They stayed together until Aldred died in 1963.[24]

Ironically, though it came close to Aldred's ideal, the union of Milly Witcop – Rose's older sister – and Rudolf Rocker was one that Guy often criticized. Milly had been the first of her family to come to London in 1894, when she was only fifteen. She worked hard to save enough to bring over her entire family in 1897, and she had, by that time, become actively involved with East End Jewish radicals. Rudolf Rocker was a German who emigrated to France and then England. His family was Social Democratic and opposed Prussianism in Germany; he turned to anarchism after becoming involved with Jewish anarchists during his stay in Paris.

He lived with a woman named Charlotte in Germany and France, and they had a son together in 1893. They did not remain together, though, since they had, in Rocker's words, 'no spiritual bond'. Rocker came to England in 1895, and he devoted himself to the workers in the Jewish East End, where he met Witcop. The two quickly became a couple, despite being different from each other both physically and emotionally. None of their differences seemed to matter; in the words of a Spanish anarchist friend, they were 'the romantic pair.'[25]

Rocker and Witcop's views of marriage were fairly typical of anarchists of this time. Their beliefs came out most clearly when they tried to emigrate to the United States in 1898. They registered as a married couple so that they could have a cabin together, but they intended this to be temporary only. When they arrived in New York in May, they stopped the pretense, thus leading to a confrontation with the immigration officials. The officials asked for their marriage certificate, and Rudolf told them that they had no such papers. According to his memoir, he then explained, 'Our bond is one of free agreement between my wife and myself. It is a purely private matter that concerns only ourselves, and it needs no confirmation from the law.' One female official then asked Milly how, as a woman, she could agree with such a notion, since it would allow Rocker to desert her whenever he wished to do so. Milly replied that she would not consider it 'dignified as a woman and a human being' to keep a man who did not love her by her side. The woman, horrified, told Milly that such attitudes would lead to 'free love.' Milly replied, 'Love is always free ... When love ceases to be free, it becomes prostitution.' Unsurprisingly, this remark ended the conversation. The immigration authorities ultimately told the couple that they must marry or leave the country. Rocker and Witcop chose to return to England rather than submit to this requirement, a stand that gave them brief notoriety both in America and England.[26]

Rocker and Witcop worked together in an unmarried partnership during the next several years, and their union exemplified the notion of equality and freedom in private life that many anarchists considered essential. At some points Rudolf was unable to support them from his earnings as a leader of the Jewish radicals, and Milly's work as a dressmaker supplemented their income. She also committed her savings to helping relaunch the *Arbeter Fraint*, an anarchist newspaper, in addition to helping set the type for all his publications. They had one son, Fermin, and also took in Rudolf's son with Charlotte when the boy was six years old. In contrast to

Rose, Milly had no interest in other men, whether or not she and Rudolf were physically together. When Rocker was interned in World War I, Milly stuck by him until she herself was arrested in 1916. They saw each other only twice in four years, yet when she was offered a chance to go to Russia with Fermin, but without Rudolf, in 1918, Milly refused. She would not leave England without him. Rocker was finally released in March 1918, but he had temporarily lost his German citizenship, so he ended up in Amsterdam. He wrote to the Home Secretary to request Milly's release, and she and Fermin joined him in the autumn of 1918. The Rockers lived in Europe until 1933, when the Nazis caused them to flee Germany, and, for the second time, they emigrated to the United States. In order to get into the country, they finally married in Germany – thirty-five years after first refusing to do so.[27]

Witcop and Rocker were a devoted pair both before and after the legal ceremony. They shared a passionate commitment to anarchism and socialism, and Witcop's support made Rocker's work possible. Rocker's belief and practice of equality was also important to the success of the partnership. According to William Fishman, Rocker's approach to leadership was to treat 'all ages and sexes' equally: 'Unlike most ideologues, Rocker lived out his conviction that, in every sense, relations between the sexes should be free, and without artifice.'[28] Though Milly was more responsible for domestic tasks, Rocker acknowledged her tireless help in his publishing and organizing work as well. After her death in 1955, Rocker wrote a tribute to her that was touching in its romantic tone:

> There was much that I was able to give Milly and she accepted it with gratitude. She, on the other hand, gave me far more in return. She opened a door in my heart which had been unknown to me before and which might never have been opened without her. Through the open door came sunshine, came joyous experience and inner peace without which life would be hopelessly distorted. This is why she will always be with me ... She was a part, and surely the best part of my life.[29]

In other words, in this case, the ritual did not seem to matter one way or the other. They were happy unmarried, but also happy married; the crucial aspect was their devotion to each other. As Rocker put it, '[t]he worst enemies of happiness have been those who have sought to impose their formula of happiness on others.

Happiness that is forced upon one is nothing but gilded slavery. There is no happiness without free choice.'[30] Thirty-five years of unmarried bliss was followed by twenty-two years of the married variety. Whatever their legal status, they always considered themselves married. They referred to each other and 'husband' and 'wife', and Milly sometimes used Rudolf's last name. Aldred criticized them for this, but free choice surely meant being able to choose to live in a free union on one's own terms, even if they resembled legal marriage. Yet if free unions followed all the customs of marriage, what was the advantage of the former? Rocker explained: 'Milly was a person with an inherent sense of responsibility, such as one seldom finds, and it is precisely for this reason that she was a truly free human being in everything she thought and did.'[31] Though Milly left few writings of her own, none of the evidence from the time indicates that Rudolf's view of their relationship was incorrect. He probably idealized her, but the longevity of their partnership and its survival against many odds indicates that he was substantially truthful. Indeed, Aldred's clear envy of their happiness indicates that they managed to get closer to free love than Guy managed with Rose.

Naturally, Rocker and Milly did not have everything their own way; as with Guy and Rose, their social situation was not supportive of marital experimentation. The union caused similar ripple effects in family relationships. Milly's mother was not happy with her free union, and this led to some strain, though her parents were also upset with her atheism and radical politics, so would have been distressed in any case. But the main problem came from Guy, who resented both Milly's union and that of her sister Polly, who lived with a married man named Simmerling. Aldred complained that Mrs. Witcop was prejudiced against him because the two older daughters were already in relationships with 'married' men (Aldred mistakenly believed Rocker had married in France). He was annoyed at being put in the same category as Rocker and Milly who, he insisted, were living in free unions from convenience rather than principle. In addition, Milly disliked Aldred and tried to separate him from Rose early on in their affair. Aldred put this down to hypocrisy, but probably she disliked Guy's judgmental attitude. All the same, even these differences were smoothed over. When Guy went to prison, Milly offered help, and Rose returned the favor when Rudolf was interned, so the sisters became reconciled. And, in contrast to the negative effects on some family members, the happiness of the Rocker union made other relationships better. Milly offered a loving home to Rudolf's son with Charlotte, for example. In addition, like many radicals, Rudolf and Milly had an alternative family in their close-knit group of comrades, particularly after the publicity of their refusal to marry in America.[32]

CONCLUSION

As these two contrasting unions demonstrate, anarchist couples faced the dilemma of what freedom meant squarely. If one should be free to do as one wished, did this preclude legal marriage? Or should the right to bind oneself also be included in the list of freedoms? Eventually both of these couples did marry, yet little changed in their domestic lives. Rudolf and Milly continued to be happy, and Guy and Rose continued to live apart. Perhaps resistance to marriage was less necessary than all four had originally believed. The real issue was to determine how far sexual license should go. Rose insisted on her sexual freedom while Guy was in prison, but that choice had repercussions, especially for Aldred. Rocker and Milly preferred to be faithful, even if they theoretically accepted sexual freedom. This too was consistent with anarchism since limiting one's sexual partners was also a choice.

Ironically, the group most associated with the bugbear of 'free love' (in the sense of meaning sexual promiscuity by both partners) actually did not often practice this kind of freedom. Male anarchists did not like the idea of women being 'common property,' because it contradicted their feminist beliefs. Women anarchists, for their part, feared desertion or male promiscuity. The couples under review here largely concurred with that consensus. Guy, Rudolf, and (presumably) Milly disapproved of uncommitted sexual relations. Rocker, for example, wanted to expel male members of his organization who had sex with and then abandoned women members, believing them to have perverted anarchist ideas for the sake of their own sexual satisfaction. Other anarchists went further. Since Guy believed in the perfectability of humanity, he assumed those 'animal' parts of human nature would disappear in time, which was one reason he was ambivalent about all sexual relationships. And though he tended to fanaticism, Aldred was sometimes right about other anarchist couples. One comrade of Rocker's, a man named Tchishikoff, lived with a young girl named Zlatke, got her pregnant, and then threw her out of his house when his legal wife arrived from Russia. Similarly, Rose and Milly's sister Polly lost her lover when his legal wife arrived in England; consequently, she arranged a quick marriage of convenience. Such examples show the remaining dangers to women of a belief in 'freedom' without a corresponding belief in responsibility.[33]

The issue of feminism was also vexed. Though the anarchists were more consistent about women's sexual freedom than many socialist groups, even their challenge to social convention had its limits. Milly worked as hard as Rudolf to earn money and keep their cause going, but she still did most of the housekeeping and child-rearing. This was typical of anarchists as a whole. Peter Kropotkin published bold calls to men to stop seeing women as 'drudges', yet, as Hermia Oliver put it, 'Sophie [his wife] cooked the dinner.' Similarly, in the anarchist communal experiment at Whiteway, domestic chores were the responsibility of women only.[34] The point of contention relates to that of sexuality, of course. One reason that women continued to do most domestic labour was that they bore children and had smaller earnings than their male counterparts. Thus, they faced more difficulties when unions failed, making 'free love' particularly problematic for them, as Polly discovered. Rose was unusual in being able to surmount that difficulty with apparent ease; little wonder that she favored birth control. In addition, the gender differences interacted with class. Despite the challenges, anarchists coped with the issues of women's sexuality and the position of children more easily than groups like the organized women's movement. Property issues and respectability were much less important for them; since they had little property to pass down to children, illegitimacy was not a huge concern. And they had no interest at all in appearing respectable or attracting well-off supporters in Parliament. Again, this class advantage helped a women like Rose, who did not bother marrying the father of her child for seventeen years.

In the end, both of these couples encountered significant constraints, and both apparently compromised their principles to marry. As long as the state gave great advantages to those legally married, the choice not to marry entailed penalties that were hard to ignore. Milly and Rudolf married to enable them to live in the US, while Aldred gave his protection to Rose to prevent her deportation. At times, marriage was convenient or even necessary while society remained unreformed. When one believed in individual development and happiness, one also had an obligation to make sure one's partner had the same opportunity. This obligation inevitably brought limits to freedom in its train, as did the necessity to support children. In short, individual freedoms and the freedom of others sometimes clashed. To his credit, Guy made sure that Rose would be able to flourish in her adopted country, even if it meant sacrificing some of his ideals.

Less creditable was the tendency to moralize personal choices, for example, Aldred's claim that his union with Rose was 'purer' and more idealistic than others. Anarchists' different responses to questions of promiscuity, fidelity and issues of custom – whether to wear rings, share names and so forth – provided ample opportunity to elevate some choices over others. Nor did many of them include homosexual partnerships in their analyses; most made no mention at all of the possibility, and some condemned it. At times, anarchists were as moralistic as the Victorians they disdained, Aldred being a case in point. These attitudes were neither inevitable nor surprising, since they sprang from the idealism that sparked the experiments in the first place.

Nevertheless, in their willingness to try to solve such problems, anarchists also foreshadowed many of the legal and social reforms of the later twentieth century. In particular, the loosening of divorce laws followed the anarchists' (and others') insistence that commitments could only last as long as the affection between the parties did. Forcing unhappy partners to remain together became a thing of the past, particularly with the coming of no-fault divorce. In addition, the arguments that anarchists made about women's liberation were also borne out in the legal changes in women's status throughout the twentieth century, though there is still some way to go. The welfare state has helped eliminate some, though not all, of the economic concerns for single parents, particularly mothers. Marriage has not disappeared, but it is no longer the only choice for family formation, as the number of cohabiting couples continues to rise.[35]

Yet, like the successes, the dilemmas that anarchists faced in the early 1900s remain. Marriage continues to confer advantages on both parties, for example, with pension support in old age. In fact, some cohabiting couples choose to marry late in life in order to be able to get all their benefits. And no legal system can adjudicate fairly between a partner who prefers monogamy and life-long commitment and one who does not. Most modern legal processes favor the freedom of the individual who prefers to leave, rather than the wishes of the other. This is probably the only option, but, as Guy Aldred could attest, such choices leave scars. Some couples do reach close to the ideal, as did Milly and Rudolf, but those couples would be happy whether married or not. Nellie Shaw summarized the position well in her conclusions about the free unions and marriages at Whiteway:

> It can be truly said that free unions compare quite favourably with legal marriage in the way they work out. But at the same time I cannot claim that they are much better ... Some free union couples exhibit as much exclusive, exacting property sense as any orthodoxly married couple could. And conversely, many married people show a fine spirit of liberty in their relationship. The matter is, after all, more a question of temperament than anything else.[36]

On the issue of free unions, then, were these anarchists overly optimistic, as many critics alleged? Or did they simply envision a better world, one that was distinctly possible? Unlike the leaders of many social justice movements, some anarchists challenged the marital regime in actions as well as words, putting their theories to the test. Naturally, not all proved valid; for instance, Aldred's belief that celibacy would become the norm as humans 'evolved,' did not pan out in his own life or beyond. Other ideas were impossible just for that time period. Neither Guy nor Rudolf managed to avoid entanglements with the state, despite their best efforts, since the political and economic context militated against them. Instead, both worked out practical ways to build partnerships, adapting to circumstances as necessary. The experience of living in free unions mitigated anarchists' 'utopian' rhetoric about marriage. These two cases showed that though anarchists wanted a better world, their yearning did not leave them unable to adapt their principles to suit the circumstances in which they found themselves. The variety of approaches, indeed, showed that one solution could not fit all situations, even within a single lifetime. This flexibility was the main ally of anarchists in making love 'freer' for both partners.

ENDNOTES

1. Peter Shipley, *Revolutionaries in Modern Britain* (London: The Bodley Head, 1976), 172-76; W. C. H., *Confessions of an Anarchist* (London: Grant Richards, 1911), 89-98.

2. Hermia Oliver, *The International Anarchist Movement in Late Victorian London* (London: Croom Helm, 1983); John Quail, *The Slow Burning Fuse: The Lost History of British Anarchists* (London: Paladin, 1978), 19-21, 47-61; George Cores, *Personal Recollections of the Anarchist Past* (London: Kate Sharpley Library, 1992); Nellie Shaw, *Whiteway; A Colony in the Cotswolds* (London: C.W. Daniel Company, 1935); Joy Thacker, *Whiteway Colony: The Social History of a Tolstoyan Community* (Stroud, Gloucestershire: Alan Sutton Publishing, 1993). For a fictionalized account of Anarchist émigrés, see Isabel Meredith, *A Girl Among the Anarchists* (Lincoln, Nebraska: University of Nebraska Press, 1992 [first published 1903]).
3. Lucy Bland, *Banishing the Beast: Sexuality and the Early Feminists* (New York: The Free Press, 1995), 124-85, quote from 133; Barbara Caine, *English Feminism, 1780-1980* (Oxford: Oxford Univesity Press, 1997), 134-47; Margaret Jackson, *The Real Facts of Life: Feminism and the Politics of Sexuality, c. 1850-1940* (London: Taylor & Francis, 1994), 1-33; Philippa Levine, *Feminist Lives in Victorian England: Private Roles and Public Commitment* (Oxford: Basil Blackwell, 1900), 79-102.
4. Barbara Taylor, *Eve and the New Jerusalem: Socialism and Feminism in the Nineteenth Century* (Cambridge, Mass.: Harvard University Press, 1993), 183-216; Friedrich Engels, *Origin of the Family, Private Property, and the State* (New York: International Publishers, 1973 [first published 1884]), 96-145.
5. Karen Hunt, *Equivocal Feminists: The Social Democratic Federation and the Woman Question, 1884-1911* (Cambridge: Cambridge University Press, 1996), 23-36; Christine Collette, 'Socialism and Scandal: The Sexual Politics of the Early Labour Movement,' *History Workshop Journal* 23 (1987), 102-111; Jane Lewis, 'Intimate Relations Between Men and Women: The Case of H.G. Wells and Amber Pember Reeves,' *History Workshop Journal* 37 (1994), 76-98.
6. Fox quoted in Guy Aldred, *No Traitor's Gait! The Autobiography of Guy A. Aldred* 3 vols. (Glasgow: Strickland Press, 1957-63), II: 318; W. C. H., *Confessions*, 133 (for second quote).
7. Verax, 'The Logic of Free-Love,' *The Anarchist* 1, #7 N.S. (October 1886), 4-5, quote from 4; Shaw, *Whiteway*, 128.
8. W.C.H., *Confessions*, 133; Shaw, *Whiteway*, 128; Henry Seymour, 'The Anarchy of Love,' *The Anarchist* 2, #5 N.S. (1 July 1888), 3, 6; 'The Anarchy of Love,' *The Anarchist* 2, #6 N.S. (1 August 1888), 3, 6-7, quote from 7.
9. Aldred, *No Traitor's Gait!*, II:309-320; John Taylor Caldwell, *Come Dungeons Dark:*

The Life and Times of Guy Aldred, Glasgow Anarchist (Barr, Ayrshire: Luath Press, Ltd., 1988), 9-24, 55-57; Aldred, *From Anglican Boy Preacher to Anarchist Socialist Impossibilist* (London: Bakunin Press, 1908), 46. See also Quail, *A Slow Burning Fuse*, 241-42; 248-49; 280-83.

10. Aldred, *From Anglican Boy Preacher to Anarchist*, 48-52.
11. Aldred, *No Traitor's Gait!*, II:372; Aldred, 'Questions of Sex-Oppression,' *Freewoman* 2 (18 July 1912), 179.
12. Guy Aldred, 'Labour and Malthusian Heresy,' *Voice of Labour* 1 (13 July 1907), 138; 'Socialism, Women, and the Suffrage,' *Voice of Labour* 1 (27 July 1907), 146-47; 'Socialism, Women, and the Suffrage,' *Voice of Labour* 1 (3 August 1907), 150; *The Religion and Economics of Sex Oppression* (London: Bakunin Press, 1907), 26-32 (for last quote).
13. Aldred, *No Traitor's Gait!*, II:328, 353, 372; Aldred, *From Anglican Boy Preacher to Anarchist*, 46; 'Socialism, Women, and Suffrage,' 150.
14. Aldred, *From Anglican Boy Preacher to Anarchist*, 52, 46; Aldred, *Religion and Economics of Sex Oppression*, 36-40.
15. Aldred, *No Traitor's Gait!*, II:313-16; 399, 403 (for quote); Rose Witcop, 'Correspondence,' *Voice of Labour* 1 (2 March 1907), 51; Rose Witcop, 'A Retort,' *The Freewoman* 1 (22 February 1912), 273.
16. Aldred, *No Traitor's Gait!*, II: 403-406; 423-31; III:443; Caldwell, *Come Dungeon's Dark*, 201-207 (quote on 201).
17. Aldred, *No Traitor's Gait!*, II:320-23; 372-74, 399.
18. Ibid., II:327, 424.
19. Ibid., II: 328, 399, 403; Caldwell, *Come Dungeons Dark*, 84-85; 102-103.
20. Aldred, *No Traitor's Gait!*, III:444.
21. Ibid., II:327.
22. Ibid., II:385.
23. Ibid., II:400.
24. Aldred, *No Traitor's Gate!*, 385-97; Caldwell, *Come Dungeons Dark*, 221-34.
25. Rudolf Rocker, *The London Years* (London: Robert Anscombe & Co., 1956), 98-101; William Fishman, *East End Jewish Radicals, 1875-1914* (London: Duckworth & Company, 1975), 229-37; Mina Grauer, *An Anarchist 'Rabbi': The Life and Teachings of Rudolf Rocker* (New York: St. Martin's Press, 1997), 42-43; 74-77.
26. Rocker, *The London Years*, 101-105; Grauer, *An Anarchist 'Rabbi'*, 77-78.

27. Rocker, *The London Years*, 249-359; Grauer, *An Anarchist 'Rabbi'*, 92-93; 127-39; 175-76; 208-212; Oliver, *The International Anarchist Movement*, 141-43.
28. Fishman, *East End Jewish Radicals*, 268.
29. Rudolf Rocker, *Milly Witcop Rocker* (Orkney, UK: Ciefuegos Press, 1956), 19.
30. Ibid., 10.
31. Rocker, *Milly Witcop Rocker*, 9; Aldred, *No Traitor's Gait!*, II:399.
32. Aldred, *No Traitor's Gate!*, II:320; Rocker, *The London Years*, 98, 318. For another example of a happy anarchist couple in the Jewish East End, see R. M. Fox, *Drifting Men* (London: Hogarth Press, 1930), 53-55.
33. Fishman, *East End Jewish Radicals*, 270; Aldred, *No Traitor's Gait!*, II:320.
34. Oliver, *The International Anarchist Movement*, 153; Shaw, *Whiteway*, 47-89.
35. Jane Lewis, *The End of Marriage? Individualism and Intimate Relations* (Cheltenham, UK: Edward Elgar, 2001), 29-42.
36. Shaw, *Whiteway*, 131.

Anarchist Studies 17.1 © 2009 ISSN 0976 3393
www.lwbooks.co.uk/journals/anarchiststudies/

REVIEW ARTICLES

The political legacy of Murray Bookchin

Ever since I read *Post-Scarcity Anarchism* some thirty years ago I have been a fan of Murray Bookchin – in the same way that I have been a fan of Peter Kropotkin, Richard Jefferies, Elisee Reclus and Ernest Thompson Seton. All were pioneer ecologists. In 1981 in a review of a book on eco-philosophy, I described Bookchin as a 'lone voice crying in the wilderness', and even ten years later still felt the need to publish an essay on 'The Social Ecology of Murray Bookchin' (1996: 131-138), emphasizing Bookchin's seminal importance as a social ecologist and as a radical political thinker. However, by the end of the decade, Bookchin's trenchant (and valid) criticisms of deep ecology, anarcho-primitivism and the bourgeois individualism of the likes of Hakim Bey, had thrust Bookchin into the media limelight, and he became something of a controversial figure. He certainly ruffled many feathers, especially amongst those happily ensconced in the academy. He thus came to be assailed from all sides – by deep ecologists, political liberals, technophobes, spiritual ecologists, anarcho-primitivists, poetic terrorists, neo-Marxists and Stirnerite individualists, as well as by the acolytes of Nietzsche and Heidegger.

In the process, of course, Bookchin's seminal importance as a social ecologist and as a radical anarchist thinker tended to be forgotten, if not completely denigrated. But what to me was important about Murray Bookchin was that he re-affirmed and creatively developed the revolutionary anarchist tradition that stemmed essentially from Michael Bakunin, Peter Kropotkin and Elisée Reclus. This tradition emphasized the need to integrate an ecological world view or philosophy – what Bookchin was later to describe as dialectical naturalism – with the political philosophy offered by anarchism, that is, by libertarian socialism. This political tradition and social movement, as many have emphasized, combined the best of both liberalism, with its emphasis on liberty and individual freedom, and socialism with its emphasis on equality, voluntary associations, mutual aid and direct action. This unity, that indeed defines libertarian socialism (or anarchism), was most succinctly expressed in the well-known maxim of Michael Bakunin: 'That liberty without socialism is privilege and injustice, and that socialism without liberty is slavery and brutality' (Lehning 1973: 110).

Some forty or so years ago Murray Bookchin sensed that the social and the natural must be grasped in a new unity, that the time had come to integrate an ecological, natural philosophy (social ecology) with the social philosophy based on freedom and mutual aid (anarchism or libertarian socialism). This unity was essential, he argued, if we were to avoid an ecological catastrophe. What we must therefore do, Bookchin stressed, was to 'decentralize, restore bioregional forms of production and food cultivation, diversify our technologies, scale them to human dimensions, and establish face-to-face forms of democracy', as well as to foster a 'new sensibility toward the biosphere' (1980: 27).

Although in later years Bookchin became embroiled in rather acrimonious debates with deep ecologists, anarcho-primitivists and bourgeois individualists – in which Bookchin fervently defended his own brand of social ecology and libertarian socialism – Bookchin never, in fact, deviated from the views he expressed in his earlier writings. Bookchin's core ideas on social ecology, libertarian socialism and libertarian municipalism – which he defended and elaborated upon throughout his life – are thus to be found in three key early texts, namely, *Post-Scarcity Anarchism (*1971), *Toward an Ecological Society* (1980) and his magnum opus *Ecology of Freedom* (1982). As Tom Cahill remarked in his generous tribute to Bookchin, these books contain the 'essence' of Bookchin's thoughts (2006: 164).

It has to be recognized that although Bookchin always expressed his views with some stridency, even rancour – to a degree that many found disturbing – he was in fact no more doctrinaire, sectarian and ideological than the anarcho-primitivists and the individualist anarchists with whom he disputed, and he expressed a much broader social vision. What could be more narrow and sectarian than the kind of anarcho-primitivism expressed by Bob Black and Jolhum Zerzan? Uri Gordon, deeply offended by Bookchin's 'vituperative attacks' on the 'new anarchists', thus comes to completely ignore the substance of Bookchin's critique (2008: 26), for anyone who has read, for example, the esoteric writings of Hakim Bey (a.k.a. Pete Lamborn Wilson) can easily understand why Bookchin described them as 'narcissistic', 'elitist', 'petit-bourgeois' and as a 'credo for social indifference' (1995: 20-26). Benjamin Franks is of the same opinion. For Franks suggests that

Bey's kind of bourgeois politics completely fails to confront the oppressive power of both the state and capital, happily co-existing with them, and is essentially a form of liberalism, akin, he even suggests, to anarcho-capitalism (2006: 266-67). And contrary to what many academics think, the anarcho-capitalism of the likes of Ayn Rand – 'Aynarchism', as Ruth Kinna (2005: 25) describes it – is not by any stretch of the imagination anarchist as Bookchin described it. (See my critique of Ayn Rand's politics 1996: 183-192). Bey is just an old-fashioned liberal with a penchant for Nietzschean aesthetics and Islamic mysticism, and his liberal politics were rightly condemned by Bookchin.

What Bookchin describes and critiques as 'life-style' anarchism is in fact what many academics have now come to describe as the 'new anarchism' (e.g. Kinna 2005, Curran 2006). According to Ruth Kinna (2005) this 'new anarchism' consists of a rather esoteric pastiche of five ideological categories – for Bookchin can in no sense be described as a 'new' or 'life-style' anarchist! These categories are: the anarcho-primitivism associated with Bob Black and John Zerzan; the 'poetic terrorism' of Hakim Bey and John Moore who follow the aristocratic aesthetic nihilism of Friedrich Nietzsche; Stirnerite individualism; the anarcho-capitalism of Murray Rothbard and Ayn Rand; and, finally, the so-called post-modern anarchism that is derived from the writings of Deleuze, Foucault, Derrida and Lyotard. None of this 'new anarchism' is in fact either new or original. What they have in common is the kind of radical individualism and neo-romanticism that Bookchin identified and critiqued as 'life-style' anarchism.

In their response to Bookchin's critique, Bob Black, David Watson and, surprisingly, John Clark (a.k.a. Max Cafard, who at one time was a fervent devotee of Bookchin) all harshly denounce Bookchin's social ecology, and were more than a match for Bookchin in their invective. Bookchin thus came to be depicted by these three as an aspiring 'anarchist Lenin', an 'anarcho-leftist fundamentalist', a dogmatic 'technocrat' and advocate of 'spontaneous violence' due to Bookchin's 'revolutionary fantasies', the arrogant promoter of some 'Faustian project', as well as being described as an intellectual buffoon. Bookchin's defence of reason and truth – as against religious dogma, mysticism and postmodern relativism – implied, it was argued, that he had affinities to the American neo-conservatives, advocates of free market capitalism! (Watson 1996, Black 1997, Clark 1998)

Although Robert Graham (2000) has little sympathy with the acrimonious and denunciatory polemics that have marred the anarchist debates around social ecology – and rightly so – he nevertheless defends Bookchin's integrity, and suggests that the three critics have seriously misjudged, or wilfully misinterpreted, Bookchin's social ecology.

In the bookshops now is a useful little book entitled *Social Ecology and Communalism* (2007). In many ways it constitutes Bookchin's last testament, and provides a good introduction and summary of Murray Bookchin's political legacy. It consists of four essays written in the last decades of his life, and has a short but useful introduction by the editor Eirik Eigland.

The first essay 'What is Social Ecology?', originally published in 1993, essentially outlines Bookchin's thoughts on the emergence of hierarchy and capitalism, and his conception of an ecological society. For Bookchin, human life is essentially a paradox. For on the one hand, humans are intrinsically a part of nature, the product of an evolutionary process. That humans are conceived as 'aliens' or as 'parasites' on earth, as suggested by some deep ecologists and eco-phenomenologists, Bookchin found quite deplorable. It implied, he argued, a 'denaturing of humanity', and denies the fact that humans are 'rooted' in biology and evolutionary history.

On the other hand, in the course of their development as a unique species-being, humans have developed language, a potential for subjectivity and flexibility, and a 'second nature', such that their cultures are rich in experience and knowledge. This gives humans technical foresight, and the capacity to creatively refashion their environment (pp.24-7).

To understand the natural world as an evolutionary process, and the place of humans within the cosmos, Bookchin therefore argues that we need to develop an organic way of thinking, one that is dialectical and processual, rather than instrumental and analytic. Such a way of thinking avoids the extremes of both anthropocentrism, exemplified by Cartesian metaphysics which radically separates humans from nature, and biocentrism, which is a naïve form of biological reductionism expressed by both deep ecologists and sociobiologists (pp.27-8).

Early human societies, Bookchin argued, were essentially egalitarian, practising mutual aid and following the principles of usufruct and the 'irreducible minimum' – the notion that everyone in a community was entitled to a basic livelihood (p.37). Bookchin goes on to suggest that the first forms of hierarchy were based on age and gender and that it is therefore important to make a distinction between hierarchy as a form of domination and class exploitation (p.36).

Although the idea of dominating nature is almost as old as that of hierarchy itself, Bookchin emphasizes that the current ecological crisis has its roots not in over-population, technology or human nature, but in the capitalist system, which is inherently anti-ecological. It is well to recall that over forty years ago Bookchin was reporting in detail the environmental and health costs of pesticides, food additives, chemicalized agriculture, pollution, urbanization and nuclear power. He was even, with some prescience – long before Al Gore and George Monbiot – highlighting the problems of global warming – that the growing blanket of carbon-dioxide would lead to destructive storm patterns, and eventually the melting of the ice caps and rising sea levels (1971: 60). But the cause of this ecological crisis, for Bookchin, was not because humans were inherently the most destructive parasite on earth; rather it was due to a capitalist system that was in its very essence geared to exploitation, competition and to ruthless economic expansion. This is spelled out in the second essay, 'Radical Politics in an era of Advanced Capitalism', where Bookchin describes capitalism as an 'ecological cancer', a form of 'barbarism' that is making the earth virtually unsuitable for complex forms of life (p.56). Equally important, for Bookchin, is that capitalism is not simply an economic system that is polluting and ravaging the natural world; it is also leading to the expansion of commodity relationships into all areas of social and cultural life. One thing that can be said about Bookchin is that he is a fervent anti-capitalist, in ways that media radicals like Naomi Klein and George Monbiot are most certainly not. For both Klein and Monbiot are simply reformist liberals, with a vision of some benign forms of capitalism.

This leads Bookchin to advocate the creation of an 'ecological society', involving the following: the social transformation of society along ecological lines; the elimination of class exploitation and all forms of hierarchy and domination; a spiritual renewal that develops humanity's potential for rationality, foresight and creativity; and the fostering of an ecological sensibility and what Bookchin describes as an 'ethics of complementarity ' (pp.46-7). But crucial to Bookchin's vision of an ecological society is the need to develop a radical form of politics based on the municipality.

Unlike Nietzschean 'free spirits' and Stirnerite individualists, who in elitist fashion rely on other mortals to provide them with the basic necessities of life, Bookchin recognized that throughout human history some form of social organization has always been evident. For humans are always intrinsically social beings. Some kind of organization has therefore always been essential, not only in terms of human survival, but specifically in terms of the care and upbringing of children (kinship), in the production of food, shelter, clothing and the basic necessities of human life (the social economy) and finally, in the management of human affairs, relating to community decisions and the resolution of conflicts (politics). Bookchin, therefore, has always been keen to distinguish between ordinary *social* life, focussed around family-life and kinship, affinity groups and productive activities, and the *political* life of a community, focussed around local assemblies.

Bookchin has been equally insistent on distinguishing between *politics* – which he defined as a theory relating to the public realm and to those social institutions by means of which people democratically managed their own community affairs – and what he called 'statecraft'. The latter was focussed on the state, defined as a form of government that served as an instrument for class exploitation and for class oppression and control (p.95). Thus Bookchin saw 'government' – institutions which deal with the problems of orderly social life – as consisting of two forms: as the state, or as local democratic assemblies centred on what he described as municipal politics.

But even in his earliest writings, reflected in the seminal essay *The Forms of Freedom*, Bookchin was concerned with exploring what 'social forms' were most consistent with the 'fullest realization of personal and social freedom' (1974: 143). It is of interest that in this early essay Bookchin is critical of the limitations of workers' councils and does not in fact use the term 'government', only that of 'self-management'. He also indicated the dangers of an assembly becoming an 'incipient state' (p.168).

In his last essays, however, Bookchin argues that we need a new politics based on what he describes as the 'communalist project'. As in the early writings, he describes the various forms of popular assemblies that have emerged throughout European history, particularly during times of social revolution. Bookchin is particularly enthusiastic about the classical Athenian *polis*, where citizens managed the affairs of the community through a form of direct democracy, instituted in a popular assembly (even though, as Bookchin always recognized and stressed, such a form of democracy was marred by patriarchy, slavery and class rule – p.49). The Athenian *polis* was in fact a city-state. But such forms of popular democracy had been found from earliest times, and Bookchin cites, for example, the following: the popular assemblies of medieval towns; the neighbourhood *sections* formed during the French revolution; the Paris commune of 1871; the workers' soviets during the Russian revolution; and the New England town meetings (p.49).

Bookchin thus comes to put a focal emphasis on the need to establish popular democratic assemblies, based on neighbourhoods, towns and villages. Such local assemblies through face-to-face democracy, would make policy decisions relating to the management of community affairs (p.101). He argues consistently that such decisions should be made by majority vote, though Bookchin does not advocate majority rule (p.109), and emphasizes that a free society would only be one that fosters the fullest degree of dissent and liberty. He is, however, given his early experiences with the anti-nuclear Clamshell Alliance, highly critical of consensus politics, except for small groups (p.110).

But Bookchin goes on to argue that such local or municipal assemblies must be formally structured, with constitutions and explicit regulations (p.111), and that the assembly, as the sole policy-making body, has priority over the workers' committees and the co-operatives concerned with food production and other social activities. These would have a purely administrative function. As Bookchin puts it: 'Every productive enterprise falls under the purview of the local assembly, which decides how it will function to meet the interests of the community as a whole' (2007: 103). Town and neighbourhood assemblies would be linked through confederal councils, consisting of mandated delegates sent by the assemblies (p.50). It seems important for Bookchin that power be both decentralized, and instituted in local communities, organized through face-to-face democratic assemblies. Even more controversial, Bookchin advocates that communalists, i.e. libertarian socialists, should not hesitate to run candidates in local government elections, and thereby attempt to convert them to popular assemblies (p.115).

What has troubled many anarchists is that while the 'life-style' or 'new' anarchists have, as ultra-individualists, denigrated or even repudiated the socialist component of anarchism – derided as 'leftism' (that is, they have repudiated political protest and class struggle) – Bookchin in his later years, partly in reaction to the 'life-style' anarchists, has moved to the other extreme and has increasingly downplayed not only cultural protest, but the libertarian aspect of anarchism. Thus his emphasis on local assemblies and confederations as structured institutions that take priority not only over voluntary associations and self-management of the economy, but also, it seems, over the individual, seems to many to introduce an element of hierarchy quite foreign to anarchism, that is, libertarian socialism or anarchist communism. In fact, the whole idea of 'government' seems contrary to anarchist principles

Bookchin has always acknowledged the importance of protests and struggles to achieve a better world – whether centred around nuclear power, ecological issues, health care and education, or community issues, as well as the importance of the anti-globalization movement in challenging capitalism, both on cultural and economic grounds (p.85). Nevertheless, Bookchin has tended to focus 'direct action' rather narrowly on local municipal *elections*. This also seems contrary to libertarian socialist principles, for local authorities are essential appendages of the nation-state. This strategy is thus basically reformist.

Bookchin's critique of 'life-style' or 'new' anarchism is, I think, largely justified and valid. In fact, the essay 'The Role of Social Ecology in a Period of Reaction' is largely devoted to a reaffirmation of what was expressed in his controversial polemic *Social Anarchism or Lifestyle Anarchism* (1995). For besides emphasizing that social ecology is deeply rooted in the ideals of the radical Enlightenment and the revolutionary socialist tradition (p.71), Bookchin argues that the 'new' or 'lifestyle' anarchism, as expressed by the likes of Hakim Bey, Bob Black and Jason McQuinn, is largely a retrogressive 'goulash' in its embrace of spiritualism, anti-rationalism, primitivism and bourgeois individualism. Lifestyle anarchism, he writes, with some derision, is little more than an ideology that panders to petit bourgeois tastes in eccentricity (p.72).

Thus his hostility towards 'life-style' anarchism and radical individualism, combined with his advocacy of a highly structured form of municipal 'government' (no less) has led Bookchin to almost forget the libertarian component of anarchism and the cultural importance of the concepts of individual freedom and autonomy, both personal and social, as well as of cultural revolt. Indeed, in his early writings Bookchin put a crucial emphasis on the self, on self-activity and self-management, arguing that a truly free society does not deny selfhood and individual freedom, but rather supports and actualizes it (1980: 48). He even advocates life-style politics as being an indispensable aspect of the revolutionary project (1974: 16). But as Robert Graham (2004) has argued, Bookchin's later writings on 'communalism', with its focus almost exclusively on the structured municipal assembly, tends to downplay or marginalize direct action, the self-management of the economy, and the crucial importance of individual freedom. Anarchism has a dual heritage, and must not only be socialist (denied by most of the 'new' or life-style anarchists) but also libertarian – which seems to be rather downplayed by Bookchin in his last years.

It has to be recognized, of course, that although Bookchin is highly critical of Marxism and the idea of a 'proletarian revolution', as well as of anarcho-syndicalism given his hostility to the 'factory system', Bookchin never repudiated the concept of the 'class'. He always acknowledged – as a fervent anti-capitalist – the crucial importance of the working class in achieving any form of social revolution, and categorically affirmed the importance of class struggle (1999: 264).

It is also important to note that although Bookchin was a harsh critic of the kind of anarcho-primitivism that essentially stemmed from the writings of Fredy Perlman, he was not an obsessive 'technocrat' as portrayed by Watson (1996) – in fact Bookchin described himself as a bit of a Luddite. Nor was he besotted with civilization. He certainly emphasized the importance of the city, especially in introducing the idea of a common *humanitas* (61); but like both Peter Kropotkin and Lewis Mumford – both important influences on Bookchin – and unlike the anarcho-primitivists, Bookchin had a much more nuanced approach to both technology and civilization. As he put it, in defending his pro-technology stand: '[this] is not to deny that many technologies are inherently domineering and ecologically dangerous, or to assert that civilization has been an unmitigated blessing. Nuclear reactors, huge dams, highly centralized industrial complexes, the factory system, and the arms industry – like bureaucracy, urban blight and contemporary media – have been pernicious almost from their conception' (1995: 34).

Following Kropotkin, Bookchin therefore came to emphasize that there had been two sides to human history – a legacy of domination reflected in the emergence of hierarchy, state power and capitalism, and a legacy of freedom, reflected in the history of ever-expanding struggles for emancipation (1999: 278).

It is thus disheartening to read, in the last essay, on 'The Communalist Project', that Bookchin comes to deny that he is an anarchist; that he had embraced, as an alternative, the politics of 'communalism'. Rather ironically, communalism is defined as a form of libertarian socialism, and is seen as the political dimension of social ecology, libertarian municipalism being its praxis (p.108).

Significantly, making clear demarcations between Marxism, anarcho-syndicalism and anarchism, Bookchin comes to define anarchism narrowly in terms only of its individualistic tendency. Thus in both the essay, and in his preface to the third edition of *Post-Scarcity Anarchism* (2004), Bookchin comes to define anarchism as a 'tangle of highly confused individualistic concepts'. Anarchism is thus misleadingly interpreted in terms of 'life-style' anarchism, characterized by ultra-individualism, nihilism, mutualism, aestheticism, and as being radically opposed to any form of organization. Both conceptually and historically this is an inaccurate depiction of anarchism, which has always embraced a dual heritage of liberty and socialism. But it leads Bookchin – like the Marxists, anarcho-primitivists and Stirnerite egoists – to postulate a false and quite untenable dichotomy between anarchism and socialism. For historically the main strand of anarchism has been anarchist-communism (or libertarian socialism), combining liberalism – as existential not possessive, individualism – with socialism. The socialism that Bookchin now espouses as communalism, which he affirms as both libertarian and revolutionary (p.96), is in fact good old-fashioned anarchism. First formulated by Bakunin towards the end of the nineteenth century, anarchism in this sense has various synonyms: anarchist-communism, revolutionary anarchism, libertarian communism, class struggle anarchism, or as Bookchin and many contemporary anarchists conceive it: social anarchism or libertarian socialism.

Authentic anarchism is not then the life-style (or 'new') anarchism – as Bookchin contended in his last years – but the class struggle anarchism embraced by Reclus, Kropotkin, Goldman, Berkman, Flores Magon, Galleani, Malatesta, Landauer and by scores of contemporary anarchists and radical activists who muster (at least in Britain) under such banners as Class War, the Solidarity Federation (the Direct Action Movement), Black Flag, Industrial Workers of the World and the Anarchist (Communist) Federation (see Franks 2006). Bookchin, in spite of his rhetoric, and in spite of misleadingly equating anarchism with ultra-individualism, always essentially belonged to this libertarian socialist tradition – anarchism. Bookchin's true legacy, it seems to me, was in re-affirming and creatively developing this tradition, not in advocating libertarian municipalism, with its rather reformist implications.

Brian Morris
Emeritus Professor of Anthropology, Goldsmiths' College London

REFERENCES

Black, B. (1997), *Anarchy After Leftism,* Columbia; CAL Press

Bookchin, M. (1974), *Post-Scarcity Anarchism,* London: Wildwood House

(1980), *Toward an Ecological Society,* Montreal: Black Rose

(1995), *Social Anarchism or Lifestyle Anarchism,* Edinburgh: AK Press

(1999), *Anarchism, Marxism and the Future of the Left,* Edinburgh: AK Press

(2007), *Social Ecology and Communalism,* Edinburgh: AK Press

Cahill, T. (2006), Murray Bookchin (1921 – 2006), *Anarchist Studies* 14/2: 163 – 66

Clark, J. (1998), Municipal Dreams in A. Light (Ed), *Social Ecology After Bookchin,* New York: Guildford Press

Curran, G. (2006), *21st Century Dissent,* Basingstoke: Palgrave

Franks, B. (2006), *Rebel Alliances,* Edinburgh: AK Press

Gordon, U. (2008), *Anarchy Alive!* London: Pluto Press

Graham, R. (2000), Broken Promises: The Politics of Social Ecology Revisited. *Social Anarchism:* 29: 26-41

(2004), Re-Inventing Hierarchy: The Political Theory of Social Ecology. *Anarchist Studies.* 12/1: 16-35

Kinna, R. (2005), *Anarchism: a Beginners Guide,* Oxford: Oneworld Publ.

Lehning, A. (Ed) (1973), *Michael Bakunin: Selected Writings,* London: Cape

Morris, B. (1996), *Ecology and Anarchism,* Malvern Wells: Images

Watson, D. (1996), *Beyond Bookchin,* Brooklyn NY: Autonomedia

Anarchist Studies 17.1 © 2009 ISSN 0976 3393
www.lwbooks.co.uk/journals/anarchiststudies/

Sex bombs: anticipating a free society

Free Comrades: Anarchism and Homosexuality in the United States, 1895-1917

Terence Kissack

AK Press, Edinburgh, 2008
ISBN 978-1904-859116
229pp.+index £14

Edward Carpenter: A Life of Liberty and Love

Sheila Rowbotham

Verso, London, 2008
ISBN 978-1-84467-295-0
565pp. £25

At first sight Oscar Wilde and Edward Carpenter make unlikely bedfellows. In their own lifetimes they were international celebrities renowned for their lifestyles as much as their writings, but while Wilde has remained so, Carpenter is now best known (if at all) as a forerunner of gay liberation. Both challenged the conventions of late-Victorian England, but they constructed their sexual, political, and artistic identities very differently. A characteristic photograph of Carpenter shows him outside his rural home, bearded and sandaled: in his rough-and-ready clothes he looks as if he has just been gardening. Wilde's carefully posed publicity photographs are taken in a studio, where he demonstrates his dandified elegance, his distance from everyday life. The images of the two men, like their writings, appear to epitomise the contrast between nature and artifice, simplicity and ornament, seriousness and wit, the direct and the elusive. These contrasts correspond to two persistent versions of sexual identity: as nature, authenticity, truth, bespeaking an innermost self – or as mask, pose, style, a playing with the idea of self.

In the 1970s, the Gay Liberation Movement claimed them as forerunners: Wilde the martyred hero, Carpenter the brave pioneer. Carpenter's writings on sexuality were rediscovered and republished. However, as Terence Kissack points out in *Free Comrades*, the rediscovery of the work of nineteenth and early twentieth century sex radicals has too often ignored its wider political context. He argues that anarchists made a unique contribution to the development of a politics of homosexuality, incorporating it in a vision of social transformation. Speaking out when others were silent, they helped to spread new ideas about human nature and sex. Anglophone anarchists in the USA participated in a transatlantic debate about the moral, ethical and social place of homosexuality.

Carpenter was an important figure in this debate: an influential sex radical, he was, according to Sheila Rowbotham's comprehensive biography, someone who 'helped to prod the modern world into being ... among the first to challenge capitalism as a social and economic system, linking external transformation with new forms of relating and desiring', and developing 'a flexible version of socialism with anarchist stripes which put the emphasis on changing everyday living and behaviour'.[1]

Socialism with anarchist stripes can, looked at from another perspective, be anarchism with socialist stripes. Can Carpenter and Wilde be claimed as anarchists? In the early 1890s at the height of the 'anarchist scare' when anarchism, in the popular press, was nearly synonymous with dynamite, both men publicly said that they were. Neither supported violent 'propaganda by deed', but each gave practical as well as moral assistance to accused and imprisoned anarchists. At other times they described their beliefs differently, or refused categorisation; perhaps, as with the notion of sexual identity, what is important about a political identity is how it is used, what kind of politics it makes possible.

Kissack argues that for anarchist sex radicals, Wilde's 1895 trial and imprisonment for homosexuality functioned as a powerful symbol of state enforcement of sexual norms. Anarchist feminist critiques of marriage, sexuality and gender relations had already opened up a space for the defence of same-sex love, and the dissident culture of anarchism encouraged challenges to social taboos. Anarchists were among the very few who spoke out publicly in Wilde's defence. For Emma Goldman, among others, he was not just a victim, he was a revolutionary who used his art to attack bourgeois morality. In the ensuing years, anarchists published, republished, and quoted his work, making it part of their own history.

Not all anarchists thought that sexuality was important, and even those that did could be homophobic. But Kissack shows how anarchism enabled an approach to homosexuality far more open than anything coming from the conventional left or conservative feminism. One of the strengths of his book is his analysis of the different understandings of homosexuality among anarchists, and how their ideas changed over time and in different contexts.

Sexology, the new science of sex, promised a rational approach free from religious moralising, and Goldman adapted sexological ideas to discuss homosexuals as members of a persecuted minority, similar to other oppressed groups. Individualist anarchist Ben Tucker took a different approach, using a discourse of individual rights to argue for free sexual relationships between consenting individuals, regardless of gender. Opposing censorship, he claimed that 'there is no desire ... whose satisfaction is so fraught with evil consequences to mankind as the desire to rule'. The eclectic anarchist William Lloyd anticipated some of today's Queer politics in his vision of an eroticised spectrum of human relations, a 'larger love' which allows for a diversity of desires, without limitations on the gender or number of partners. He looked forward to a future when 'there will be strange love-groups and anomalous families different from any now seen or deemed possible'. As Carpenter said of the New Women of the 1890s: 'Sometimes it seems possible that a new sex is on the make.'[2]

The subtitle of Carpenter's *The Intermediate Sex*, first published in 1908, is 'A study of some transitional types of men and women'. Arguing that there is a natural continuum of gender and sexual characteristics, and that Intermediates often combine the most positive features of masculinity and femininity, he draws on Whitman's notion of comradeship to envision a sexual democracy of equals, the basis of a transformed society. The transition is not just between Man and Woman, but between present and future. Rowbotham notes that his views on gender and sexuality were not always consistent, but the daring exploration of ideas, the giving voice to un-named desires, and above all his positive attitude, were far more important to most of his readers than theoretical consistency.

Increased public awareness and discussion of homosexuality were liberating, but also led to more vigorous policing of the boundaries between heterosexuality and homosexuality. It became harder to inhabit the safe spaces of ambiguity where censorship and prosecution might be avoided, and Lloyd was just one of those who ended up trying to dissociate himself from any possible imputation of homosexuality. Although Kissack does not develop the point, sex radicals who were gay had good reason to feel more vulnerable than others when speaking out publicly on the subject. (A fuller discussion of specific laws concerning sexual behaviour and obscenity, and their impact, would have been a useful addition to his book.)

Carpenter, though he struggled to get some of his work published in the aftermath of the Wilde trial, excelled in what Rowbotham calls a careful frankness. He lived openly with his male lover for over forty years, and wrote repeatedly and positively about same sex love in accessible language, gaining a wide readership. For Carpenter, love, including sexual love, inspires and energises the work that needs to be done to transform the world. 'When a new desire has declared itself within the human heart ... then the revolutions of nations are already decided, and histories unwritten are written', he wrote in his best-selling prose-poem *Towards Democracy*. In a series of pamphlets later reworked as *Love's Coming of Age*, he linked women's emancipation, same sex relationships, sexual love and the creation of a free society. 'Sex bombs', commented his friend, feminist author Edith Ellis – who years later, on a lecture tour in the USA, not only spoke about homosexuality but came out as a lesbian – her own bombshell, exploding the barrier between public and private.[3]

'You are always in my heart. Mx' reads the inscription inside my copy of the 1911 edition of *Love's Coming of Age*. That was its seventh edition: the book was another international success. By 1906 it included the chapter on the intermediate sex which had been refused by the publisher a decade earlier, in the aftermath of the Wilde trial. The original pamphlet had been 'for private circulation' only. But print runs, large or small, tell only part of the story. Sexual dissidents found ways to circulate restricted or banned materials. The reading and exchange of books is one of the cultural guerrilla tactics by which subversive ideas are disseminated. Given as gifts between friends and lovers, often with underlinings and asterisks beside significant passages, books connect their readers both literally and symbolically in an imagined community.

There was no overt lesbian or gay movement as such in Britain or the USA in this period, but Rowbotham suggests that as Carpenter became better known he played a covert organisational role through his extensive international correspondence with people from all over the world, many of whom wrote to ask for his advice and support in changing their lives. Pilgrims trekked to Millthorpe, the smallholding outside Sheffield where, with his companion George Merrill and others, Carpenter tried to exemplify co-operation, simple living and the free life. Rejecting asceticism and dogmatism, he aimed to inspire experimentation rather than laying down a blueprint.

In 1912, Emma Goldman's magazine *Mother Earth* ran a special offer for its readers. Five dollars would get them, in one bargain bundle, Berkman's *Prison Memoirs*, Proudhon's *What is Property?*, Frank Harris's *The Bomb*, Kropotkin's *Russian Literature* and Carpenter's *Love's Coming of Age*. Berkman's and Carpenter's books both discuss same sex love and sexuality extensively and sympathetically, and whatever the practical considerations behind the particular selection of books, it suggests the potential for interconnections between different aspects of anarchist thought. As Lloyd wrote: 'the "Democracy" of which [Carpenter] prophesies and chants is the "Anarchy" of Kropotkin, the "institution of the dear love of comrades" of Whitman, the "fellowship" which is the "life" of Morris – the world of emancipated men [sic], free and loving'.[4] Such synthesising approaches, combining anarchism as critique, as culture, as resistance and prefiguration, reflect the utopian spirit of the period, a desire that all of life should be changed.

If one man could embody all this, it was Carpenter. Rowbotham's beautifully written biography skilfully creates a vivid picture of the complex intersecting milieux in which new ideas were emerging, new movements flourishing, new kinds of lives being lived. Carpenter's writings may now be of mainly historical interest, but how he practised his politics has continuing relevance. He was a breaker or more precisely an ignorer of boundaries, an 'epistemological rover', in Rowbotham's phrase, who drew on both science and mysticism to write about alternative ways of knowing as well as alternative ways of living. He thought revolutionaries should not sacrifice the present for the future, and that small changes were worthwhile. His 'lifestyle' politics emphasised nature, bodily freedom (after travelling to India, he added making and selling sandals to the activities at Millthorpe – freedom from the constraint of the Victorian boot!) – and the importance of the everyday. The startling radicalism of some of his ideas was camouflaged by the moderate tone in which they were expressed. He tried to avoid destructive arguments and sectarianism, building bridges, finding middle ground, opening up spaces for conversation and the cross-fertilisation of ideas. Drawing on the utopian energies of his times, 'he picked up shifts which were less explicit than concepts, called them desires, and somehow cleared space for them to come into being'.[5] Without being prescriptive, he tried to imagine and put into practice alternative ways of living. He was influential because of his ability to voice unspoken feelings, make connections, foster networks, across a wide range of cultural and political groupings.

Drawing on an impressive range of scholarly materials to produce accessible and thought-provoking analysis, both Kissack and Rowbotham aim to do more than acknowledge and honour these figures from the past. Both take pains to contextualise their subjects. In Kissack's shorter book, context primarily means the American anarchist movement, with some interesting comparisons with the attitudes of other radicals and revolutionaries; his work provides a valuable foundation and inspiration for further research. Rowbotham places Carpenter more fully within a complex period of rapid social change, when the utopian ideas of one moment might become the commonsense or the lost cause of another.

Kissack uses his research to suggest that historians of anarchism, the left and gay movements all need to engage with the interaction between anarchism and the politics of homosexuality. Emphasising that an understanding of sexual politics is essential to any project of social transformation, he urges today's sex radicals to aim not for integration but for a fundamental restructuring of society.

Rowbotham deploys her research to suggest that the best way to transmit revolutionary ideas is to concentrate on communication and inspiration rather than aiming for ideological correctness at all times: pragmatism is more useful than dogmatism. While Kissack concentrates on the public pronouncements rather than the private lives of the figures he discusses, Rowbotham, though always alert to the methodological problems involved, investigates both. She brings out the problems and tensions, the residual prejudices and blind spots, the painful muddles and disagreements which are inevitably part of transformatory projects – not to denigrate such projects, but to suggest the necessity of careful negotiation and self-awareness. As for contradictions, they can be seen not as indicators of an inadequate philosophy, but as signs of life, responses to changing conditions. To quote Whitman: 'Do I contradict myself? Very well then I contradict myself, (I am large, I contain multitudes.)'[6]

Emma Goldman – who did as much as anyone to make it possible to speak publicly about homosexuality – could be strikingly contradictory. Denying that

Louise Michel was a lesbian, she criticised what she saw as gay people's misguided attempts to claim notable individuals for their 'creed'. On the other hand, she was happy to claim Havelock Ellis as an anarchist, even after he denied it. But identifying oneself or someone else as an anarchist, or as gay, need not turn into a debate about the truth of some inner state of being. Such identifications (or disavowals) are political acts. Historical evidence is important, but raises as many questions as answers.

Whitman's expansive notion of self anticipates Wilde's and Carpenter's enactments of identity, and the ways in which these have been interpreted. Rowbotham notes that Carpenter's project of exemplifying his politics in his personal life disguises as well as reveals the 'private self'. The photograph of Carpenter at Millthorpe is just as carefully posed as Wilde's in the studio: neither are expressions of identity, but messages about possible ways of being – of acting – in the world.

Judy Greenway
University of East London

NOTES

1. Rowbotham 1.
2. Kissack 74, 84; Rowbotham 215.
3. Kissack mentions the lecture tour only to quote an unfavourable contemporary comparison with Emma Goldman. He describes Edith only as the wife of Havelock Ellis (and his discussion of the latter in the context of English anarchism is rather shaky). There are also a number of typos, and readers who want to track down Nechaev, Lord Douglas, Audre Lorde, or Radclyffe Hall should beware of the sound-alikes in the text. These are, though, small defects in an otherwise thorough, scholarly, and readable work.
4. Kissack 80.
5. Rowbotham 253, 105.
6. Walt Whitman (1855), 'Song of Myself' in *Leaves of Grass*, 1940, Doubleday: New York.

Anarchist Studies 17.1 © 2009 ISSN 0976 3393
www.lwbooks.co.uk/journals/anarchiststudies/

REVIEWS

Durruti in the Spanish Revolution

Abel Paz

AK Press, Oakland, CA./Edinburgh
ISBN 978-1-904859-50-5; $27.50/£20

This is the definitive version of Diego Camacho's (a.k.a. Abel Paz) monumental biography of Buenaventura Durruti, the celebrated activist who most embodied the heroism, resistance and spirit of sacrifice of the Spanish anarchist movement. But it is more than a simple biography: it is a history of a mass movement, of its fight to establish a space for itself in society, and of its role in the revolution of 1936 and its evolution during the civil war. As such, it is an important study of the Spanish anarchist movement refracted through the life of one its most famous sons.

The book itself has a long history: it first appeared in French in 1962, only appearing in Spanish in 1978, three years after the death of Franco and his censorship. (Earlier editions have been translated into Italian, German, Portuguese, English and Japanese.) This tome supersedes the first English edition (1977) in two key respects: unlike its predecessor, it benefits from an elegant and erudite translation by Chuck Morse; and most crucially, it was only in 1996, some 34 years after the appearance of the first edition, that Camacho concluded his research on Durruti, publishing the fully-revised and complete Spanish version of the biography. Almost 800 pages long, the current volume is the fruit of decades of research in archives and libraries, not to mention extensive interviews with Durruti's former comrades and family members. Camacho, who like his subject, emigrated to Barcelona from a poor background, is an ideal biographer: now in his 90s, his entire life has been interwoven with the libertarian movement - he was educated in rationalist schools, graduated to militancy in the CNT, enjoyed the heady days of revolution in 1936, before going on to finishing school in exile and French concentration camps.

Durruti's odyssey, concentrated into 40 intense years of life, is breathtaking and picturesque. Born on 14 July 1896 in the relatively conservative city of León, his early life was very similar to that of thousands of other working-class children. He was the second eldest of 8 brothers, and was exposed to poverty, injustice and repression from an early age: when just 7 years old, Durruti's father, a tanner, was detained after participating in a strike movement. The young Buenaventura was ineluctably drawn into union activity. Given that León was a socialist stronghold, his first activism was in the reformist UGT, from which, most tellingly, he was expelled for employing direct action during a strike in 1917. This resulted in his first period of exile in France, where he entered into contact with Spanish anarchist émigrés.

Upon his return to Spain, in 1919, he joined the CNT. These were the boom years of Spanish revolutionary syndicalism, a time of violent class struggle, as the bourgeoisie, haunted by the spectre of the Russian Revolution, sought to hold onto its position of authority in the factories with a broad gamut of union-busting tactics, including lock-outs, state-organised death squads, internment without trial and blacklisting of militants, and so on. With the CNT effectively placed outside the law, anarcho-syndicalist and anarchist militants responded with expropriations to fund the unions and the growing cost of supporting prisoners and their families, and by assassinating politicians and employers most clearly associated with the repression. In this context, Durruti and his comrades gained notoriety in Spain as 'men of action' and urban guerrillas *avant la lettre*, initiating a series of high profile *attentats* and expropriations, such as that in Gijón, in September 1923, at the time the most lucrative bank raid in Spanish history. When General Primo de Rivera launched a coup d'état that same month, Durruti and his closest associates found it prudent to go into exile, leaving for the Americas and the Caribbean, where they blazed a trail across much of the region during 1924-26, launching *attentats* and expropriations, including the first bank robbery in Chile's history. While certainly some money was used to cover their own living and legal expenses, most of the proceeds of these expropriations went to bolster the anarchist and union movements in Europe and the Americas. Durruti and his allies worked when possible, being employed, for instance, on the Havana docks during their time in Cuba. Pursued by the authorities in several south American countries, and with a death sentence hanging over him in Argentine, Durruti returned to Europe in 1926, finding work in a Renault factory in Paris, where he met Nestor Makhno. That same year Durruti was implicated in a foiled assassination attempt on King Alfonso XIII during a state visit to the French capital, a move he calculated would shake the foundations of Spain's monarchist dictatorship. Once arrested, only a broad mobilisation in France stymied extradition attempts by several foreign governments, including those of Spain, Argentina and Cuba.

With the birth of the Republic in 1931 Durruti was able to return to Spain, whereupon he was identified with the most radical positions within the anarchist movement, and resisted attempts to incorporate the unions within the new democracy. During these years he acquired mythical status, inspiring fear and admiration in equal measure among his enemies and supporters alike, and was heavily involved in the cycle of armed insurrections against the Republic. In a movement that was marked by a far from insignificant degree of machismo, Durruti periodically rebuked the sexism of his comrades. Blacklisted, it often fell to his partner to find paid work, while he occupied himself with domestic work, cleaning and cooking, and looking after the children. He played a very active role in the street fighting that put down the 1936 coup that prefaced the revolution at the start of the civil war. This was a victory tinged with a tremendous personal tragedy for Durruti, who witnessed the death of Francisco Ascaso, his long-standing comrade in arms, in the course of the armed assault on the Atarazanas army barracks in downtown Barcelona.

With the revolution in full flow in the rearguard, Durruti led a militia column, the celebrated Durruti Column, which initially consisted of around 2,500 men and women, to the Aragón front. Yet the revolution was quickly eclipsed by the war. And with the war going badly and with fascist troops entering Madrid, anarchist leaders and their anti-fascist political allies clamoured for Durruti and his militia to bolster the defence in the University area of the city. And this was where Durruti would die, on 19 November 1936, receiving a bullet to the chest as he rallied his militia to continue their resistance after days of fighting without respite. Like most of his life, his death was shrouded in controversy and speculation. Some have claimed that the fatal bullet originated from within the ranks of his militia by those hostile to alleged plans to militarise the Column; others have suggested his death was part of a Stalinist provocation. The controversy surrounding Durruti's death is treated rigorously over some 70 pages in the final section of the book. What we can be sure of is that Durruti's funeral prompted an outpouring of collective grief in Barcelona, as around half a million people thronged the streets in what was the largest ever attendance at a funeral in the city's history.

In death, Durruti's legacy was appropriated by the hierarchy of the anarchist movement; he was converted into a symbol of the war effort to justify their possibilism, their prioritisation of anti-fascist struggle over the revolution, and their participation in republican state institutions. This was encapsulated in the much-quoted expression attributed falsely to Durruti: 'We renounce everything except victory'. But a figure like Durruti was not easily shorn of his revolutionary content. While the anarchist leaders performed pirouettes in government, up until the point that they were of no further use to their erstwhile cabinet 'allies', it was no coincidence that the most strident and vocal opponents to libertarian reformism should call themselves 'The Friends of Durruti' in the spring of 1937. And, indeed, the example of Durruti has continued to inspire future generations across the globe, something that can only be enhanced by the appearance of this new study.

Chris Ealham
Saint Louis University, Madrid

Getting Free: Creating an Association of Democratic Autonomous Neighborhoods

James Herod

Lucy Parsons Center, Boston 2007 (AK Distribution)
164 pp., online at www.jamesherod.info

This is a rewritten and updated edition of James Herod's counter-power manifesto, originally published (in photocopy) in 1998, and since then revised in three Internet editions under the name of Jared James.

Getting Free is a succinct and straightforward polemic, whose aim is 'to persuade revolutionaries to shift the sites of the anticapitalist struggle and to select new battlefields' – neighbourhoods, workplaces, and households – there 'to build the life that we want, and then fight to defend this life and our social creations from attacks by the ruling class' (1). The proposed strategy is therefore dedicated to 'gutting capitalism' by building alternative institutions for collective social life based on direct democracy.

Herod briefly presents a vision of a libertarian socialist society built of associated households, projects, peer circles and neighbourhood assemblies. He then gives quite short shift to a series of 'strategies that have failed', from Leninism, syndicalism and insurrections to single-issue campaigns, new social movements, dropping out, luddism, publishing and education (24-37). Some of these are rejected entirely; others 'should be subordinated to the main task'.

The alternative strategy is to '*stop participating* in activities that support (finance, condone) the capitalist world and *start participating* in activities that build a new world while simultaneously undermining the old' (p.38). Presented next, again in short sections, are 'ways to begin gutting capitalism': forming neighbourhood, employee and housing associations, worker-owned businesses, local currencies, community land trusts and sustainable energy/food sources. Other proposals include resisting construction projects; supporting alternative media and unschooling; not becoming a soldier, a cop or a boss; beginning to break away from the nuclear family; and actively refusing elections.

While Herod offers diverse practical possibilities, he does not grapple at much length or depth with many of the questions that trouble his strategy. To the most serious one – that it presupposes an already-existing, widespread anti-capitalist consciousness – he responds with rather empty appeals to 'think strategically' and reclaim a sense of historical agency (92-4). Yet it remains unclear how the exemplary but sparse projects initiated by a sensitized anarchist minority are supposed to grow into a mass movement that consciously resists capitalism. Nor does the text anywhere address the converging crises of oil scarcity, climate change and financial collapse, which cast serious doubt on the viability of any gradual counter-power strategy.

A further issue of concern is that *Getting Free*, strongly inspired as it is by the writings of direct democrats such as Murray Bookchin and Takis Fotopoulos, mirrors their almost republican preoccupation with rational public deliberation, investing the act of formal assembly with more revolutionary significance than it deserves. Sadly, Herod quite confusedly dismisses feminists' criticisms of the masculine and ultimately authoritarian logic that is privileged here over more informal, invisible and liberatory forms of collective power.

Perhaps future editions will better address these difficulties. In the meantime, *Getting Free* nevertheless remains a valuable source for enriching and sharpening anarchist discussions of strategies for social change.

Uri Gordon
Arava Institute for Environmental Studies

Wobblies & Zapatistas: Conversations on Anarchism, Marxism and Radical History

Staughton Lynd & Andrej Grubacic

Oakland, CA: PM Press, 2008. 261 pp.
ISBN: 978-1-60486-041-2. US$20.00. Paperback

Wobblies & Zapatistas is an ambitious and well-intentioned book that promises much but in the end, unfortunately, delivers very little. The subtitle suggests a collection of conversations between Andrej Grubacic, a younger intellectual who is esteemed in anarchist circles but not as well known outside of them; and Staughton Lynd, a veteran Marxian activist much revered on the American Left for his work in the civil rights, labor, and anti-war movements. In fact, the book offers nothing of the sort, but instead reads very much like a series of interviews, with Grubacic asking the questions and Lynd providing the answers. Worse still, it often comes across as very valedictory, even hagiographic, if only because such a disproportionate amount of space is devoted to anecdotes about Lynd's career as an activist. (The point isn't that Lynd's career isn't extremely impressive – who would doubt that? – but that such details would be more at home in an autobiography than in a book about 'anarchism, Marxism, and radical history.')

Strangely, it is almost as though Grubacic himself shares my concerns. Although he repeatedly broaches the subject of anarchism throughout the book in sophisticated but extremely clear language, Lynd seldom seems to engage him directly. Instead, he tends to wander off into anecdotes which, though interesting without fail, often seem only distantly related to Grubacic's original question. Unlike Grubacic, moreover, Lynd's own style of writing, though not without a certain charm and romantic folksiness, tends to be extremely imprecise. For example, he repeatedly characterizes Marxism as a 'concern for economic survival' (48) or, more generally, as an analysis of the economic structures of society. This is, of course, utterly ridiculous. Most political theories have ideas about political economy – i.e., analyses of the economic structures of society – and who *isn't* concerned about economic survival? Time and again Lynd appears either reluctant or altogether unable to provide a clear definition of Marxism.

Lynd does not fare much better regarding anarchism. Very early on in the book, he makes the startling insinuation that the Haymarket anarchists were not anarchists at all (11-14). Elsewhere he continuously accuses the 'new anarchists' of being 'summit jumpers' (e.g., 47), a claim that is anachronistic if it was ever true at all. At his absolute worst, he rehearses some of the most exhausted Marxist clichés, as when he likens contemporary anarchists to the utopian socialists of the nineteenth century and impugns them for lacking a 'blueprint' for post-capitalist society, etc. Sometimes Grubacic poses absolutely brilliant questions which Lynd simply dismisses or answers circuitously. (In my view, one of the best examples of this is found on pages 98-99.)

It is precisely Grubacic's questions, by the way, that are the saving grace of this volume. Even more frustrating than Lynd's inability or unwillingness to answer these questions is Grubacic's inability or unwillingness to respond to Lynd. Because this is truly an interview, not a conversation, he just moves on to the next question. Judging by the critical and scholarly acumen of the questions, however, there is little doubt that Grubacic would have had quite a bit to say were he given adequate opportunity.

Although I believe the book fails at what it sets out to do, it is scarcely worthless. Staughton Lynd's reflections on, and anecdotes about, Zapatismo, the IWW, civil rights, liberation theology, solidarity unionism, etc. are incredibly valuable for their own sake, as are Andrej Grubacic's penetrating questions about anarchism and Marxism. The problem is that these elements do not come together to form a coherent whole. *Wobblies and Zapatistas* is not a conversation, nor even a set of interviews. On the contrary, it is a series of (mostly) unanswered questions from an anarchist cobbled together with a series of (partially) unsolicited reflections and stories from a Marxist. The result leaves very much to be desired.

Nathan Jun (nathan.jun@mwsu.edu)
Assistant Professor of Philosophy at Midwestern State University

Anarchism and Authority: A Philosophical Introduction to Classical Anarchism

Paul McLaughlin

Ashgate 2007, 202pp including index

Arguing about the nature of anarchism is a popular anarchist pastime, and Paul McLaughlin here offers a provocative intervention in that debate, in the form of a 'philosophical introduction to classical anarchism'. While I don't in the end find his answer convincing, he does a good deal of valuable work in the course of arguing for it.

According to McLaughlin, anarchism is *scepticism about authority*. That is, the defining centre of anarchism is: philosophical not (necessarily) activist; critical rather than ethical; and focussed on questioning a particular species of supposedly-legitimate power, especially as claimed by the State.

The conceptual Part I of the book draws on recent work in political and legal philosophy, especially by Richard De George and by Leslie Green, to clarify both of the main terms of McLaughlin's definition. First, the *scepticism* in question is neither Pyrrhonism (the essentially conservative suspension of judgment between competing knowledge claims) nor Descartes' strategic adoption of sceptical tropes as the first stage of his project of reconstructing knowledge. Rather, anarchist scepticism is Socratic questioning: faced with an assertion of authority, anarchists demand a justification. Second, *authority* is a form of domination (which is a species of social power, which is itself a species of power understood naturalistically as effective capacity). It is defined as involving a right to command (from the point of view of the authority-holder) and a correlative duty to obey (from the point of view of the person over whom authority is held). It is distinguished into moral, theoretical, and practical forms. McLaughlin here makes the important point that anarchism should not be understood as *anti*-authoritarianism: anarchists do not assume that all authority is unjustified; they ask for justifications where others tend to assume them, and are open to the possibility of justification. McLaughlin further argues that anarchists do typically regard, at least, parental authority and operative authority as – in principle – justifiable. The final chapter of Part I offers a neat taxonomy of attempted justifications for the authority of the state, together with brisk debunking responses.

Part II introduces some strands in the history of anarchist thought. McLaughlin identifies roots of anarchism in the Enlightenment, the French Revolution, and Left Hegelianism, and claims Godwin's *Enquiry Concerning Political Justice*, Proudhon's *What Is Property?*, and Stirner's *The Ego and Its Own* as foundational texts. The history becomes sketchier and more polemical as it gets more recent – post-modern anarchism, in particular, is treated very rapidly and unsympathetically. A concluding chapter connects the theoretical work McLaughlin has done to some questions of current politics, including globalisation and terrorism, in a more popular style than the rest of the book.

The McLaughlin thesis that anarchism is scepticism about authority is intriguing, and it's well worth having this picture of anarchism set out so clearly and precisely. But I want to raise some worries.

First, the claim that anarchism is centrally critical rather than ethical is implausible. McLaughlin gestures at the critical/ethical distinction in several different ways, and is never completely explicit about it; but if I've understood correctly, the 'ethical' he rejects is a utopian vision of anarchist possibility. He eventually claims that anarchism 'is not just non-utopian but even *anti*-utopian' (p. 171). But utopian imagination is a *form* of criticism: the utopian critic constructs an ideal alternative to current life precisely to foreground and attack what is wrong with that life. Even if McLaughlin rejects this, it's difficult to deny the utopianism of much anarchist thought. To use one of McLaughlin's own examples, William Godwin is certainly a critic of authority and a defender of individual rational judgment, but his criticism always takes place in the light of a utopian vision of future perfected humanity.[1]

Second, and more generally: I'm unclear why we need a *definition* of anarchism, whether as scepticism about authority or as anything else. Anarchism is at best a loose family-resemblance concept; individual anarchists have ranged widely over several different axes of contrast; and continuing the anarchist tradition is not a matter of accepting some list of authoritative premises or practices. Overstating slightly: there is no such thing as anarchism; there are only anarchists.[2] As an introduction to anarchism, *Anarchism and Authority* is, amongst other things, an attempt to shape future anarchist thinking. I share McLaughlin's view that such thinking will benefit from engagement with non-anarchist political philosophy, as with other disciplines, and I value the critical and conceptual work his book does. But I'm not convinced that a definition of the tradition is the right way to motivate such work.

Despite these objections, I recommend this book, and especially its first part: it's a careful, clearly-written example of what connections with the mainstream can do for anarchist philosophy.

Sam Clark
Lancaster University

NOTES

1. See further my *Living Without Domination* (Ashgate 2007).
2. 'There really is no such thing as Art. There are only artists.' – E. H. Gombrich, *The Story of Art* (pocket edn, Phaidon 2006), p. 21.

Unstable Universalities: Poststructuralism and Radical Politics

Saul Newman

Manchester University Press, 2007
ISBN 0-7190-7128-7, 216 pages

Thanks largely to the efforts of Saul Newman, we now refer to the site where poststructuralism intersects anarchist politics as 'postanarchism.' The term postanarchism appears to derive from the works of Hakim Bey, via Jason Adams (Day 160). (With an irony appropriate to our postmodern e-mail culture, it is sometimes abbreviated post-@.) The postanarchist philosophy and practice have been developed in the UK by Newman, in Canada by Richard Day, in the United States by Todd May and myself, and in Turkey by Sureyyya Evren and others associated with the post-@ journal *Siyahi*. Despite the growing popularity of postanarchism (or perhaps because of that), the term remains a lightning rod for controversy. Some critics denounce post-@ for its tendency to fetishise incomprehensible jargon. Others reject it as a desire to be done with anarchism altogether. Some see post-@ as an elitist form of high theory, disconnected from anarchist social movements. While these critiques have probably been true of some postanarchisms at some times, none of them apply to Saul Newman's excellent new book, *Unstable Universalities*.

Newman's project is an important one. Rather than simply rejecting postmodernism or embracing it uncritically, he seeks a third way, which would 'take a kind of critical distance from, or at least a measured attitude towards, postmodernity, while at the same time taking account of its very significant implications for politics today' (10). He also addresses another major issue in post-@ politics, namely the tension between an ominously totalizing consensus politics and a dangerous political fragmentation. Newman again tries to identify a viable third way, namely 'a notion of universality – an idea of a common political imaginary that transcends particular political perspectives and identities' (10-11). This is similar to what I have called the 'postmodern commons.' It is an attempt to respect vital elements of difference and diversity within the community of postmodern radicals, while simultaneously recognizing that such radicals must constitute themselves *as* a coherent community if they wish to develop an effective politics.

Newman focuses mainly on the postanarchist position, and he ably demonstrates that the meaning of postanarchism need not be obscure. 'Postanarchism is simply the attempt to renew anarchist theory and politics through a deconstruction of its original foundations in the rationalist and humanist paradigms of the Enlightenment' (195). Newman's description of the postanarchist project is clear, concise and remarkably modest. Postanarchism represents a desire to interrogate the origins of modern anarchism – not to reject the modern, but to expose the hidden tensions within it. We do this in order to gain a better understanding of the political and psychological worlds in which we operate.

In his editorial for *AS* 16.2, Newman argued that postanarchism does not see itself as being 'after' anarchism. Similarly, *Unstable Universalities* demonstrates that postanarchism is not an abandonment of the anarchist tradition; rather, it is simply the latest phase of anarchist theory. 'Post-anarchism should *not* be taken to imply a theoretical move beyond anarchism or as saying that the anarchist moment has passed' (195). Newman's analysis also indicates that postanarchism is not just a mysterious creature lurking in the high tower of theory. In fact, post-@ is thoroughly engaged with contemporary anarchist social and political movements. Newman argues convincingly that post-@ is deeply relevant to discussions of the contemporary 'security state,' but he also finds post-@ elements in the anti-globalisation movement, Zapatistism, Brazil's landless movement, anti-racist groups, and Reclaim the Streets. In this analysis, post-@ is a strikingly straightforward assessment of the symbolic and subjective environment in which contemporary anarchists operate. Newman concludes optimistically that 'perhaps anarchism ... is becoming the new "paradigm" for radical politics today' (191).

I admire Newman's optimism and enthusiasm, and I agree with him that *an* anarchist moment is arriving. However, Newman sometimes seems a little too sure that he knows the precise shape of that moment. He is right to suggest that the postmodern proliferation of identities 'does not necessarily equate with liberation' (42). Neither, however, can we assume that such an existence will *not* lead to liberation. Although he admires poststructuralism and postanarchism, Newman is surprisingly critical of posthumanism, arguing that 'these developments should not be fetishised or seen as a form of liberation, as those harbingers of the "post-human" cyber age are wont to do' (43). I have been such a harbinger in the pages of this journal, and I remain convinced that the posthuman represents a *potential* figure of liberation. Newman is right to argue that 'there is nothing emancipating, necessarily, about the disappearance of man or the loss of reality' (43), but posthumanism and simulation were always just possibilities, tactics that were useful for a time and may be again, interesting openings in the symbolic field of late modernism.

Newman's skepticism about the posthuman leads him to overlook the interesting ways in which postmodern sexualities may challenge traditional power structures. He dismisses 'a lesbian mother, an S/M practitioner, a gay preacher' as '"subject positions" which remain unpoliticised' (88). Yet Foucault observed that the homosexual was automatically at war with the state: this *is* a politicised position, and an anarchist one. The practice of S/M is based upon a careful ethical distinction between the non-consensual power which is the enemy of every anarchist, and power used consensually, for mutual erotic fulfilment. The sadomasochist could be a kind of natural anarchist.

None of these issues detract significantly from what is fundamentally a very fine book. I hope that *Unstable Universalities* will be read widely by those who love postanarchism, and by those who fear it.

Lewis Call
California Polytechnic State University

REFERENCES

Call, Lewis (2002), *Postmodern Anarchism*, Lanham, Maryland, Lexington Books. Chapter four reprints 'Anarchy in the Matrix: Postmodern Anarchism in the Novels of William Gibson and Bruce Sterling,' *Anarchist Studies* 7 (1999): 99-117.

Day, Richard J. F. (2005), *Gramsci is Dead: Anarchist Currents in the Newest Social Movements*, London, Pluto Press.

Evren, Sureyyya (6 September 2008), 'Modernity, Third World and Anarchism,' Anarchist Studies Network Conference, Loughborough University.

May, Todd (1994), *The Political Philosophy of Poststructuralist Anarchism*, University Park, The Pennsylvania State University Press.

Demanding the Impossible. A History of Anarchism

Peter Marshall

Harper Perennial, London, 2008, 3rd edition (first published 1992 by Harper Collins; published by Fontana with amendments, 1993), 818 + xv pages.
ISBN: 978-0-00-686245-1; £14.99.

The first edition(s) of this very successful book will be familiar to most if not all readers of *AS*, and there seems little point in repeating the praise that was lavished on it when it appeared 15 years ago. This new edition has basically been augmented by an epilogue of 36pp. entitled 'The Phoenix Rising' intended to support Marshall's claim that 'anarchism is even more relevant today than when *Demanding the Impossible* was first published' (p.703). Opening with an outline of the major political and economic developments of the last 15 years and the various new forms of protest and resistance which have arisen, the epilogue takes us through a number of short sections each dealing with a movement or tendency or with the work of particular individuals: anarcha-feminism; Noam Chomsky; Colin Ward and Alan Carter; post-anarchisms (Todd May, Saul Newman, Lewis Call); post-left anarchy (Alfredo M. Bonanno, Bob Black and various N. American groups); Hakim Bey and the influence of the 'Temporary Autonomous Zone' idea; primitivism (especially John Zerzan); green anarchism; social ecology; Marshall's own ideas on 'neolithic anarchy' and 'liberation ecology'; contemporary examples of 'anarchy in action'; Zapatismo; the 'Movement of Movements'; and, in an attempt to offset the rather 'Atlantic-centric' (even, I would say, Anglo-American) bias, an arguably rather tokenistic two pages on 'Anarchy around the World' ('tokenistic' in that this section is so brief and attempts to cover so much that it is very sketchy). True to his own advocacy of an 'anarchism without adjectives' (p.703), Marshall's presentation of the different movements and schools of thought is normally very even-handed, and the generally positive (though not uncritical) tone quite uplifting. The exception is his consideration of Bookchin in the later years of his life: here, Marshall has clearly become far more critical of Bookchin and indeed tells us as much. Nevertheless, this survey update is, like the first edition, impressively informative, very clearly written and extremely useful.

Dave Berry
Department of Politics, International Relations & European Studies,
Loughborough University